Behind the Scenes

THE SCHOMBURG LIBRARY OF
NINETEENTH-CENTURY BLACK WOMEN WRITERS

General Editor, Henry Louis Gates, Jr.

Titles are listed chronologically; collections that include works published over a span of years are listed according to the publication date of their initial work.

Phillis Wheatley, *The Collected Works of Phillis Wheatley*

Six Women's Slave Narratives: M. Prince; Old Elizabeth; M. J. Jackson; L. A. Delaney; K. Drumgoold; A. L. Burton

Spiritual Narratives: M. W. Stewart; J. Lee; J. A. J. Foote; V. W. Broughton

Ann Plato, *Essays*

Collected Black Women's Narratives: N. Prince; L. Picquet; B. Veney; S. K. Taylor

Frances E. W. Harper, *Complete Poems of Frances E. W. Harper*

Charlotte Forten Grimké, *The Journals of Charlotte Forten Grimké*

Mary Seacole, *Wonderful Adventures of Mrs. Seacole in Many Lands*

Harriet Jacobs, *Incidents in the Life of a Slave Girl*

Collected Black Women's Poetry, Volumes 1–4: M. E. Tucker; A. I. Menken; M. W. Fordham; P. J. Thompson; C. A. Thompson; H. C. Ray; L. A. J. Moorer; J. D. Heard; E. Bibb; M. P. Johnson; Mrs. H. Linden

Elizabeth Keckley, *Behind the Scenes. Or, Thirty Years a Slave, and Four Years in the White House*

C. W. Larison, M.D., *Silvia Dubois, A Biografy of the Slav Who Whipt Her Mistres and Gand Her Fredom*

Mrs. A. E. Johnson, *Clarence and Corinne; or, God's Way*

Octavia V. Rogers Albert, *The House of Bondage: or Charlotte Brooks and Other Slaves*

Emma Dunham Kelley, *Megda*

Anna Julia Cooper, *A Voice From the South*

Frances E. W. Harper, *Iola Leroy, or Shadows Uplifted*

Amanda Smith, *An Autobiography: The Story of the Lord's Dealings with Mrs. Amanda Smith the Colored Evangelist*

Mrs. A. E. Johnson, *The Hazeley Family*

Mrs. N. F. Mossell, *The Work of the Afro-American Woman*

Alice Dunbar-Nelson, *The Works of Alice Dunbar-Nelson*, Volumes 1–3

Emma D. Kelley-Hawkins, *Four Girls at Cottage City*

Pauline E. Hopkins, *Contending Forces: A Romance Illustrative of Negro Life North and South*

Pauline Hopkins, *The Magazine Novels of Pauline Hopkins*

Hallie Q. Brown, *Homespun Heroines and Other Women of Distinction*

Behind the Scenes.

Or,

Thirty Years a Slave,
and Four Years in the White House

ELIZABETH KECKLEY

With an Introduction by
JAMES OLNEY

New York   Oxford
OXFORD UNIVERSITY PRESS

Oxford University Press

Oxford   New York   Toronto
Delhi   Bombay   Calcutta   Madras   Karachi
Petaling Jaya   Singapore   Hong Kong   Tokyo
Nairobi   Dar es Salaam   Cape Town
Melbourne   Auckland

and associated companies in
Berlin   Ibadan

Library of Congress Cataloging-in-Publication Data

Keckley, Elizabeth, 1824–1907.
Behind the scenes. Or, thirty years a slave, and
four years in the White House.
(The Schomburg library of nineteenth-century black
women writers)
Originally published: New York: G. W. Carlton, 1868.
1. Lincoln, Abraham, 1809–1865.   2. Lincoln, Mary Todd,
1818–1882.   3. Keckley, Elizabeth, 1824–1907.   4. Slaves—
United States—Biography.   I. Title.   II. Title: Behind
the scenes.   III. Title: Thirty years a slave and four
years in the White House.   IV. Series.
E457.15.K26   1988   973.7′092′2   87-14172
ISBN 978-0-19-506084-3

Printed in the United States of America
on acid-free paper

The
Schomburg Library
of
Nineteenth-Century
Black Women Writers
is
Dedicated
in Memory
of
PAULINE AUGUSTA COLEMAN GATES

1916–1987

PUBLISHER'S NOTE

FOREWORD
In Her Own Write

Henry Louis Gates, Jr.

One muffled strain in the Silent South, a jarring chord and a vague and uncomprehended cadenza has been and still is the Negro. And of that muffled chord, the one mute and voiceless note has been the sadly expectant Black Woman, ...

The "other side" has not been represented by one who "lives there." And not many can more sensibly realize and more accurately tell the weight and the fret of the "long dull pain" than the open-eyed but hitherto voiceless Black Woman of America.

. . . as our Caucasian barristers are not to blame if they cannot *quite* put themselves in the dark man's place, neither should the dark man be wholly expected fully and adequately to reproduce the exact Voice of the Black Woman.

—ANNA JULIA COOPER, *A Voice From the South* (1892)

The birth of the Afro-American literary tradition occurred in 1773, when Phillis Wheatley published a book of poetry. Despite the fact that her book garnered for her a remarkable amount of attention, Wheatley's journey to the printer had been a most arduous one. Sometime in 1772, a young African girl walked demurely into a room in Boston to undergo an oral examination, the results of which would determine the direction of her life and work. Perhaps she was shocked upon entering the appointed room. For there, perhaps gathered in a semicircle, sat eighteen of Boston's most notable citizens. Among them were John Erving, a prominent Boston merchant; the Reverend Charles Chauncy, pastor of the Tenth Congregational Church; and John Hancock, who would later gain fame for his signature on the Declaration of Independence. At the center of this group was His Excellency, Thomas Hutchinson, governor of Massachusetts, with Andrew Oliver, his lieutenant governor, close by his side.

Why had this august group been assembled? Why had it seen fit to summon this young African girl, scarcely eighteen years old, before it? This group of "the most respectable Characters in *Boston*," as it would later define itself, had assembled to question closely the African adolescent on the slender sheaf of poems that she claimed to have "written by herself." We can only speculate on the nature of the questions posed to the fledgling poet. Perhaps they asked her to identify and explain—for all to hear—exactly who were the Greek and Latin gods and poets alluded to so frequently in her work. Perhaps they asked her to conjugate a verb in Latin or even to translate randomly selected passages from the Latin, which she and her master, John Wheatley, claimed that she "had made some Progress in." Or perhaps they asked her to recite from memory key passages from the texts of John Milton and Alexander Pope, the two poets by whom the African claimed to be most directly influenced. We do not know.

We do know, however, that the African poet's responses were more than sufficient to prompt the eighteen august gentlemen to compose, sign, and publish a two-paragraph "Attestation," an open letter "To the Publick" that prefaces Phillis Wheatley's book and that reads in part:

> We whose Names are under-written, do assure the World, that the Poems specified in the following Page, were (as we

verily believe) written by Phillis, a young Negro Girl, who
was but a few Years since, brought an uncultivated Barbarian
from *Africa,* and has ever since been, and now is, under the
Disadvantage of serving as a Slave in a Family in this Town.
She has been examined by some of the best Judges, and is
thought qualified to write them.

So important was this document in securing a publisher for
Wheatley's poems that it forms the signal element in the
prefatory matter preceding her *Poems on Various Subjects, Re-
ligious and Moral,* published in London in 1773.

Without the published "Attestation," Wheatley's publisher
claimed, few would believe that an African could possibly
have written poetry all by herself. As the eighteen put the
matter clearly in their letter, "Numbers would be ready to
suspect they were not really the Writings of Phillis." Wheatley and her master, John Wheatley, had attempted to publish
a similar volume in 1772 in Boston, but Boston publishers
had been incredulous. One year later, "Attestation" in hand,
Phillis Wheatley and her master's son, Nathaniel Wheatley,
sailed for England, where they completed arrangements for
the publication of a volume of her poems with the aid of the
Countess of Huntington and the Earl of Dartmouth.

This curious anecdote, surely one of the oddest oral examinations on record, is only a tiny part of a larger, and
even more curious, episode in the Enlightenment. Since the
beginning of the sixteenth century, Europeans had wondered aloud whether or not the African "species of men," as
they were most commonly called, *could* ever create formal
literature, could ever master "the arts and sciences." If they
could, the argument ran, then the African variety of humanity was fundamentally related to the European variety. If not,
then it seemed clear that the African was destined by nature

to be a slave. This was the burden shouldered by Phillis Wheatley when she successfully defended herself and the authorship of her book against counterclaims and doubts.

Indeed, with her successful defense, Wheatley launched two traditions at once—the black American literary tradition *and* the black woman's literary tradition. If it is extraordinary that not just one but both of these traditions were founded simultaneously by a black woman—certainly an event unique in the history of literature—it is also ironic that this important fact of common, coterminous literary origins seems to have escaped most scholars.

That the progenitor of the black literary tradition was a woman means, in the most strictly literal sense, that all subsequent black writers have evolved in a matrilinear line of descent, and that each, consciously or unconsciously, has extended and revised a canon whose foundation was the poetry of a black woman. Early black writers seem to have been keenly aware of Wheatley's founding role, even if most of her white reviewers were more concerned with the implications of her race than her gender. Jupiter Hammon, for example, whose 1760 broadside "An Evening Thought. Salvation by Christ, With Penitential Cries" was the first individual poem published by a black American, acknowledged Wheatley's influence by selecting her as the subject of his second broadside, "An Address to Miss Phillis Wheatly [*sic*], Ethiopian Poetess, in Boston," which was published at Hartford in 1778. And George Moses Horton, the second Afro-American to publish a book of poetry in English (1829), brought out in 1838 an edition of his *Poems By A Slave* bound together with Wheatley's work. Indeed, for fifty-six years, between 1773 and 1829, when Horton published *The Hope of Liberty*, Wheatley was the *only* black person to have published a book of imaginative literature in English. So central was this black woman's role in the shaping of the Afro-American literary tradition that, as one historian has maintained, the history of the reception of Phillis Wheatley's poetry *is* the history of Afro-American literary criticism. Well into the nineteenth century, Wheatley and the black literary tradition were the same entity.

But Wheatley is not the only black woman writer who stands as a pioneering figure in Afro-American literature. Just as Wheatley gave birth to the genre of black poetry, Ann Plato was the first Afro-American to publish a book of essays (1841) and Harriet E. Wilson was the first black person to publish a novel in the United States (1859).

Despite this pioneering role of black women in the tradition, however, many of their contributions before this century have been all but lost or unrecognized. As Hortense Spillers observed as recently as 1983,

> With the exception of a handful of autobiographical narratives from the nineteenth century, the black woman's realities are virtually suppressed until the period of the Harlem Renaissance and later. Essentially the black woman as artist, as intellectual spokesperson for her own cultural apprenticeship, has not existed before, for anyone. At the source of [their] own symbol-making task, [the community of black women writers] confronts, therefore, a tradition of work that is quite recent, its continuities, broken and sporadic.

Until now, it has been extraordinarily difficult to establish the formal connections between early black women's writing and that of the present, precisely because our knowledge of their work has been broken and sporadic. Phillis Wheatley, for example, while certainly the most reprinted and discussed poet in the tradition, is also one of the least understood. Ann Plato's seminal work, *Essays* (which includes biographies and poems), has not been reprinted since it was published a century and a half ago. And Harriet Wilson's *Our Nig,* her compelling novel of a black woman's expanding consciousness in a racist Northern antebellum environment, never received even *one* review or comment at a time when virtually *all* works written by black people were heralded by abolitionists as salient arguments against the existence of human slavery. Many of the books reprinted in this set experienced a similar fate, the most dreadful fate for an author: that of being ignored then relegated to the obscurity of the rare book section of a university library. We can only wonder how many other texts in the black woman's tradition have been lost to this generation of readers or remain unclassified or uncatalogued and, hence, unread.

This was not always so, however. Black women writers dominated the final decade of the nineteenth century, perhaps spurred to publish by an 1886 essay entitled "The Coming American Novelist," which was published in *Lippincott's Monthly Magazine* and written by "A Lady From Philadelphia." This pseudonymous essay argued that the "Great American Novel" would be written by a black person. Her argument is so curious that it deserves to be repeated:

> When we come to formulate our demands of the Coming American Novelist, we will agree that he must be native-born. His ancestors may come from where they will, but we must give him a birthplace and have the raising of him. Still, the longer his family has been here the better he will represent us. Suppose he should have no country but ours, no traditions but those he has learned here, no longings apart from us, no future except in our future—the orphan of the world, he finds with us his home. And with all this, suppose he refuses to be fused into that grand conglomerate we call the "American type." With us, he is not of us. He is original, he has humor, he is tender, he is passive and fiery, he has been

taught what we call justice, and he has his own opinion about it. He has suffered everything a poet, a dramatist, a novelist need suffer before he comes to have his lips anointed. And with it all he is in one sense a spectator, a little out of the race. How would these conditions go towards forming an original development? In a word, suppose the coming novelist is of African origin? When one comes to consider the subject, there is no improbability in it. One thing is certain,—our great novel will not be written by the typical American.

An atypical American, indeed. Not only would the great American novel be written by an African-American, it would be written by an African-American *woman:*

Yet farther: I have used the generic masculine pronoun because it is convenient; but Fate keeps revenge in store. It was a woman who, taking the wrongs of the African as her theme, wrote the novel that awakened the world to their reality, and why should not the coming novelist be a woman as well as an African? She—the woman of that race—has some claims on Fate which are not yet paid up.

It is these claims on fate that we seek to pay by publishing The Schomburg Library of Nineteenth-Century Black Women Writers.

This theme would be repeated by several black women authors, most notably by Anna Julia Cooper, a prototypical black feminist whose 1892 *A Voice From the South* can be considered to be one of the original texts of the black feminist movement. It was Cooper who first analyzed the fallacy of referring to "the Black man" when speaking of black people and who argued that just as white men cannot speak through the consciousness of black men, neither can black *men* "fully and adequately . . . reproduce the exact Voice of the Black Woman." Gender and race, she argues, cannot be conflated, except in the instance of a black woman's voice, and it is this voice which must be uttered and to which we must listen. As Cooper puts the matter so compellingly:

> It is not the intelligent woman vs. the ignorant woman; nor the white woman vs. the black, the brown, and the red,—it is not even the cause of woman vs. man. Nay, 'tis woman's strongest vindication for speaking that *the world needs to hear her voice*. It would be subversive of every human interest that the cry of one-half the human family be stifled. Woman in stepping from the pedestal of statue-like inactivity in the domestic shrine, and daring to think and move and speak,— to undertake to help shape, mold, and direct the thought of her age, is merely completing the circle of the world's vision. Hers is every interest that has lacked an interpreter and a defender. Her cause is linked with that of every agony that has been dumb—every wrong that needs a voice.
>
> It is no fault of man's that he has not been able to see truth from her standpoint. It does credit both to his head and heart that no greater mistakes have been committed or even wrongs perpetrated while she sat making tatting and snipping paper flowers. Man's own innate chivalry and the mutual interdependence of their interests have insured his treating her cause, in the main at least, as his own. And he is pardonably surprised and even a little chagrined, perhaps, to find his legislation not considered "perfectly lovely" in every respect. But in any case his work is only impoverished by her remaining dumb. The world has had to limp along with the wobbling gait and one-sided hesitancy of a man with one eye. Suddenly the bandage is removed from the other eye and the whole body is filled with light. It sees a circle where before it saw a segment. The darkened eye restored, every member rejoices with it.

The myopic sight of the darkened eye can only be restored when the full range of the black woman's voice, with its own special timbres and shadings, remains mute no longer.

Similarly, Victoria Earle Matthews, an author of short stories and essays, and a cofounder in 1896 of the National Association of Colored Women, wrote in her stunning essay, "The Value of Race Literature" (1895), that "when the literature of our race is developed, it will of necessity be different in all essential points of greatness, true heroism and real Christianity from what we may at the present time, for convenience, call American literature." Matthews argued that this great tradition of Afro-American literature would be the textual outlet "for the unnaturally suppressed inner lives which our people have been compelled to lead." Once these "unnaturally suppressed inner lives" of black people are unveiled, no "grander diffusion of mental light" will shine more brightly, she concludes, than that of the articulate Afro-American woman:

> And now comes the question, What part shall we women play in the Race Literature of the future? . . . within the compass of one small journal ["Woman's Era"] we have struck out a new line of departure—a journal, a record of Race interests gathered from all parts of the United States, carefully selected, moistened, winnowed and garnered by the ablest intellects of educated colored women, shrinking at no lofty theme, shirking no serious duty, aiming at every possible excellence, and determined to do their part in the future uplifting of the race.
>
> If twenty women, by their concentrated efforts in one literary movement, can meet with such success as has engendered, planned out, and so successfully consummated this convention, what much more glorious results, what wider spread success, what grander diffusion of mental light will not come forth at the bidding of the enlarged hosts of women writers, already called into being by the stimulus of your efforts?
>
> And here let me speak one word for my journalistic sisters

who have already entered the broad arena of journalism. Before the "Woman's Era" had come into existence, no one except themselves can appreciate the bitter experience and sore disappointments under which they have at all times been compelled to pursue their chosen vocations.

If their brothers of the press have had their difficulties to contend with, I am here as a sister journalist to state, from the fullness of knowledge, that their task has been an easy one compared with that of the colored woman in journalism.

Woman's part in Race Literature, as in Race building, is the most important part and has been so in all ages. . . . All through the most remote epochs she has done her share in literature. . . .

One of the most important aspects of this set is the republication of the salient texts from 1890 to 1910, which literary historians could well call "The Black Woman's Era." In addition to Mary Helen Washington's definitive edition of Cooper's *A Voice From the South,* we have reprinted two novels by Amelia Johnson, Frances Harper's *Iola Leroy,* two novels by Emma Dunham Kelley, Alice Dunbar-Nelson's two impressive collections of short stories, and Pauline Hopkins's three serialized novels as well as her monumental novel, *Contending Forces*—all published between 1890 and 1910. Indeed, black women published more works of fiction in these two decades than black men had published in the previous half century. Nevertheless, this great achievement has been ignored.

Moreover, the writings of nineteenth-century Afro-American women in general have remained buried in obscurity, accessible only in research libraries or in overpriced and poorly edited reprints. Many of these books have never been reprinted at all; in some instances only one or two copies are extant. In these works of fiction, poetry, autobiography, biography, essays, and journalism resides the mind of the nineteenth-century Afro-American woman. Until these works are made readily available to teachers and their students, a significant segment of the black tradition will remain silent.

Oxford University Press, in collaboration with the Schomburg Center for Research in Black Culture, is publishing thirty volumes of these compelling works, each of which contains an introduction by an expert in the field. The set includes such rare texts as Johnson's *The Hazeley Family* and *Clarence and Corinne*, Plato's *Essays*, the most complete edition of Phillis Wheatley's poems and letters, Emma Dunham Kelley's pioneering novel *Megda*, several previously unpublished stories and a novel by Alice Dunbar-Nelson, and the first collected volumes of Pauline Hopkins's three serialized novels and Frances Harper's poetry. We also present four volumes of poetry by such women as Mary Eliza Tucker Lambert, Adah Menken, Josephine Heard, and Maggie Johnson. Numerous slave and spiritual narratives, a newly discovered novel—*Four Girls at Cottage City*—by Emma Dunham Kelley (-Hawkins), and the first American edition of *Wonderful Adventures of Mrs. Seacole in Many Lands* are also among the texts included.

In addition to resurrecting the works of black women authors, it is our hope that this set will facilitate the resurrection of the Afro-American woman's literary tradition itself by unearthing its nineteenth-century roots. In the works of Nella Larsen and Jessie Fauset, Zora Neale Hurston and Ann Petry, Lorraine Hansberry and Gwendolyn Brooks, Paule Marshall and Toni Cade Bambara, Audre Lorde and Rita Dove, Toni Morrison and Alice Walker, Gloria Naylor and Jamaica Kincaid, these roots have branched luxuriantly. The eighteenth- and nineteenth-century authors whose works are presented in this set founded and nurtured the black women's literary tradition, which must be revived, explicated, analyzed, and debated before we can understand more completely the formal shaping of this tradition within a tradition, a coded literary universe through which, regrettably, we are only just beginning to navigate our way. As Anna Cooper said nearly one hundred years ago, we have been blinded by the loss of sight in one eye and have therefore been unable to detect the full *shape* of the Afro-American literary tradition.

Literary works configure into a tradition not because of some mystical collective unconscious determined by the biology of race or gender, but because writers read other writers and *ground* their representations of experience in models of language provided largely by other writers to whom they feel akin. It is through this mode of literary revision, amply evident in the *texts* themselves—in formal echoes, recast metaphors, even in parody—that a "tradition" emerges and defines itself.

This is formal bonding, and it is only through formal bonding that we can know a literary tradition. The collective publication of these works by black women now, for the first time, makes it possible for scholars and critics, male and female, black and white, to *demonstrate* that black women writers read, and revised, other black women writers. To demonstrate this set of formal literary relations is to demonstrate that sexuality, race, and gender are both the condition and the basis of *tradition*—but tradition as found in discrete acts of language use.

A word is in order about the history of this set. For the past decade, I have taught a course, first at Yale and then at Cornell, entitled "Black Women and Their Fictions," a course that I inherited from Toni Morrison, who developed it in the mid-1970s for Yale's Program in Afro-American Studies. Although the course was inspired by the remarkable accomplishments of black women novelists since 1970, I gradually extended its beginning date to the late nineteenth century, studying Frances Harper's *Iola Leroy* and Anna Julia Cooper's *A Voice From the South*, both published in 1892. With the discovery of Harriet E. Wilson's seminal novel, *Our Nig* (1859), and Jean Yellin's authentication of Harriet Jacobs's brilliant slave narrative, *Incidents in the Life of a Slave Girl* (1861), a survey course spanning over a century and a quarter emerged.

But the discovery of *Our Nig*, as well as the interest in nineteenth-century black women's writing that this discovery generated, convinced me that even the most curious and diligent scholars knew very little of the extensive history of the creative writings of Afro-American women before 1900. Indeed, most scholars of Afro-American literature had never even read most of the books published by black women, simply because these books—of poetry, novels, short stories, essays, and autobiography—were mostly accessible only in rare book sections of university libraries. For reasons unclear to me even today, few of these marvelous renderings of the Afro-American woman's consciousness were reprinted in the late 1960s and early 1970s, when so many other texts of the Afro-American literary tradition were resurrected from the dark and silent graveyard of the out-of-print and were reissued in facsimile editions aimed at the hungry readership for canonical texts in the nascent field of black studies.

So, with the help of several superb research assistants—including David Curtis, Nicola Shilliam, Wendy Jones, Sam Otter, Janadas Devan, Suvir Kaul, Cynthia Bond, Elizabeth Alexander, and Adele Alexander—and with the expert advice of scholars such as William Robinson, William Andrews, Mary Helen Washington, Maryemma Graham, Jean Yellin, Houston A. Baker, Jr., Richard Yarborough, Hazel Carby, Joan R. Sherman, Frances Foster, and William French, dozens of bibliographies were used to compile a list of books written or narrated by black women mostly before 1910. Without the assistance provided through this shared experience of scholarship, the scholar's true legacy, this project could not have been conceived. As the list grew, I was struck by how very many of these titles that I, for example, had never even heard of, let alone read, such as Ann Plato's *Essays*, Louisa Picquet's slave narrative, or Amelia Johnson's two novels, *Clarence and Corinne* and *The Hazeley Family*. Through our research with the Black Periodical Fiction and Poetry Project (funded by NEH and the Ford Foundation), I also realized that several novels by black women, including three works of fiction by Pauline Hopkins, had been serialized in black periodicals, but had never been collected and published as books. Nor had the several books of poetry published by black women, such as the prolific Frances E. W. Harper, been collected and edited. When I discovered still another "lost" novel by an Afro-American woman (*Four Girls at Cottage City*, published in 1898 by Emma Dunham Kelley-Hawkins), I decided to attempt to edit a collection of reprints of these works and to publish them as a "library" of black women's writings, in part so that I could read them myself.

Convincing university and trade publishers to undertake this project proved to be a difficult task. Despite the commercial success of *Our Nig* and of the several reprint series of women's works (such as Virago, the Beacon Black Women Writers Series, and Rutgers' American Women Writers Series), several presses rejected the project as "too large," "too limited," or as "commercially unviable." Only two publishers recognized the viability and the import of the project and, of these, Oxford's commitment to publish the titles simultaneously as a set made the press's offer irresistible.

While attempting to locate original copies of these exceedingly rare books, I discovered that most of the texts were housed at the Schomburg Center for Research in Black Culture, a branch of The New York Public Library, under the direction of Howard Dodson. Dodson's infectious enthusiasm for the project and his generous collaboration, as well as that of his stellar staff (especially Diana Lachatanere, Sharon Howard, Ellis Haizip, Richard Newman, and Betty Gubert), led to a joint publishing initiative that produced this set as part of the Schomburg's major fund-raising campaign. Without Dodson's foresight and generosity of spirit, the set would not have materialized. Without William P. Sisler's masterful editorship at Oxford and his staff's careful attention to detail, the set would have remained just another grand idea that tends to languish in a scholar's file cabinet.

I would also like to thank Dr. Michael Winston and Dr. Thomas C. Battle, Vice-President of Academic Affairs and the Director of the Moorland-Spingarn Research Center (respectively) at Howard University, for their unending encouragement, support, and collaboration in this project, and Esme E. Bhan at Howard for her meticulous research and bibliographical skills. In addition, I would like to acknowledge the aid of the staff at the libraries of Duke University, Cornell University (especially Tom Weissinger and Donald Eddy), the Boston Public Library, the Western Reserve Historical Society, the Library of Congress, and Yale University. Linda Robbins, Marion Osmun, Sarah Flanagan, and Gerard Case, all members of the staff at Oxford, were extraordinarily effective at coordinating, editing, and producing the various segments of each text in the set. Candy Ruck, Nina de Tar, and Phillis Molock expertly typed reams of correspondence and manuscripts connected to the project.

I would also like to express my gratitude to my colleagues who edited and introduced the individual titles in the set. Without their attention to detail, their willingness to meet strict deadlines, and their sheer enthusiasm for this project, the set could not have been published. But finally and ultimately, I would hope that the publication of the set would help to generate even more scholarly interest in the black women authors whose work is presented here. Struggling against the seemingly insurmountable barriers of racism *and* sexism, while often raising families and fulfilling full-time professional obligations, these women managed nevertheless to record their thoughts and feelings and to *testify* to all who dare read them that the will to harness the power of collective endurance and survival is the will to write.

The Schomburg Library of Nineteenth-Century Black Women Writers is dedicated in memory of Pauline Augusta Coleman Gates, who died in the spring of 1987. It was she who inspired in me the love of learning and the love of literature. I have encountered in the books of this set no will more determined, no courage more noble, no mind more sublime, no self more celebratory of the achievements of all Afro-American women, and indeed of life itself, than her own.

A NOTE FROM
THE SCHOMBURG CENTER

Howard Dodson

The Schomburg Center for Research in Black Culture, The New York Public Library, is pleased to join with Dr. Henry Louis Gates and Oxford University Press in presenting The Schomburg Library of Nineteenth-Century Black Women Writers. This thirty-volume set includes the work of a generation of black women whose writing has only been available previously in rare book collections. The materials reprinted in twenty-four of the thirty volumes are drawn from the unique holdings of the Schomburg Center.

A research unit of The New York Public Library, the Schomburg Center has been in the forefront of those institutions dedicated to collecting, preserving, and providing access to the records of the black past. In the course of its two generations of acquisition and conservation activity, the Center has amassed collections totaling more than 5 million items. They include over 100,000 bound volumes, 85,000 reels and sets of microforms, 300 manuscript collections containing some 3.5 million items, 300,000 photographs and extensive holdings of prints, sound recordings, film and videotape, newspapers, artworks, artifacts, and other book and nonbook materials. Together they vividly document the history and cultural heritages of people of African descent worldwide.

Though established some sixty-two years ago, the Center's book collections date from the sixteenth century. Its oldest item, an Ethiopian Coptic Tunic, dates from the eighth or ninth century. Rare materials, however, are most available for the nineteenth-century African-American experience. It is from these holdings that the majority of the titles selected for inclusion in this set are drawn.

The nineteenth century was a formative period in African-American literary and cultural history. Prior to the Civil War, the majority of black Americans living in the United States were held in bondage. Law and practice forbade teaching them to read or write. Even after the war, many of the impediments to learning and literary productivity remained. Nevertheless, black men and women of the nineteenth century persevered in both areas. Moreover, more African-Americans than we yet realize turned their observations, feelings, social viewpoints, and creative impulses into published works. In time, this nineteenth-century printed record included poetry, short stories, histories, novels, autobiographies, social criticism, and theology, as well as economic and philosophical treatises. Unfortunately, much of this body of literature remained, until very recently, relatively inaccessible to twentieth-century scholars, teachers, creative artists, and others interested in black life. Prior to the late 1960s, most Americans (black as well as white) had never heard of these nineteenth-century authors, much less read their works.

The civil rights and black power movements created unprecedented interest in the thought, behavior, and achievements of black people. Publishers responded by revising traditional texts, introducing the American public to a new generation of African-American writers, publishing a variety of thematic anthologies, and reprinting a plethora of "classic texts" in African-American history, literature, and art. The reprints usually appeared as individual titles or in a series of bound volumes or microform formats.

The Schomburg Center, which has a long history of supporting publishing that deals with the history and culture of Africans in diaspora, became an active participant in many of the reprint revivals of the 1960s. Since hard copies of original printed works are the preferred formats for producing facsimile reproductions, publishers frequently turned to the Schomburg Center for copies of these original titles. In addition to providing such material, Schomburg Center staff members offered advice and consultation, wrote introductions, and occasionally entered into formal copublishing arrangements in some projects.

Most of the nineteenth-century titles reprinted during the 1960s, however, were by and about black men. A few black women were included in the longer series, but works by lesser known black women were generally overlooked. The Schomburg Library of Nineteenth-Century Black Women Writers is both a corrective to these previous omissions and an important contribution to Afro-American literary history in its own right. Through this collection of volumes, the thoughts, perspectives, and creative abilities of nineteenth-century African-American women, as captured in books and pamphlets published in large part before 1910, are again being made available to the general public. The Schomburg Center is pleased to be a part of this historic endeavor.

I would like to thank Professor Gates for initiating this project. Thanks are due both to him and Mr. William P. Sisler of Oxford University Press for giving the Schomburg Center an opportunity to play such a prominent role in the set. Thanks are also due to my colleagues at The New York Public Library and the Schomburg Center, especially Dr. Vartan Gregorian, Richard De Gennaro, Paul Fasana, Betsy

Pinover, Richard Newman, Diana Lachatanere, Glenderlyn Johnson, and Harold Anderson for their assistance and support. I can think of no better way of demonstrating than in this set the role the Schomburg Center plays in assuring that the black heritage will be available for future generations.

INTRODUCTION

James Olney

Elizabeth Keckley's *Behind the Scenes. Or, Thirty Years a Slave, and Four Years in the White House* is a fascinating example of that kind of personal narrative that occupies a mixed middle ground between history and fiction. As history it is both public and private, the "four years in the White House" being, of course, years of the great national drama of the Civil War. And yet the drama of the war is all observed from "behind the scenes," as if through a chink in a stage set. Moreover, the large public history that unfolds from 1861 to 1865 is recounted in this volume only in terms of the private emotions of real-life actors in the tragic drama of the war. It is all public drama privately experienced, with the war—and slavery as the issue that precipitated it—in the background, while in the foreground are Jefferson Davis and his wife, Abraham Lincoln and Mary Todd Lincoln, and even Stephen Douglas and "Mrs. Senator Douglas." A more novelistic subject could hardly be imagined, and Elizabeth Keckley—"Lizabeth" to Mrs. Lincoln, "Madam Elizabeth" to Lincoln, "Keckley" to Mrs. Douglas, and "Lizzie" to nearly everyone else—frequently employs novelistic means to tell the story; and yet the contrary tension of actual historical events is always there to complicate, to deepen, and to enrich the narrative texture.

As a mixed production of historical narration that displays many of the conventions of sentimental fiction, *Behind the Scenes* is both typical and, at the same time, atypical of the many personal experience narratives produced by black writ-

ers in the nineteenth century. By "personal experience narratives," I mean primarily the slave narratives that had such
a large and eager audience right up to and beyond the Civil
War. The main impetus behind the slave narratives was, of
course, to provide ammunition for the abolitionist cause by
showing a Northern audience what slavery was really like—
showing it from the slave's point of view—so that a properly
outraged (because properly informed) citizenry would bring
an end to this most peculiar and most inhuman of institutions. To a degree, Keckley's description of her experience of
slavery is well within the slave narrative tradition, examples
of which can be found in her account of the unwarranted
beatings and lashings she endured and of the particular bru-
talities of "pious" slaveholders, or in her description of slave
families broken up, of parents separated from one another
and from their children, and of the vicious mixture of cru-
elty and lust that she encountered in certain white men who
held power over her. But the "slave narrative" portion of
Behind the Scenes, comprising the first three chapters of the
book and covering the *Thirty Years a Slave* segment of the
subtitle, occupies no more than about one-eighth of the total
volume. This fact makes it quite unlike such a book as the
*Narrative of the Life of Frederick Douglass, An American Slave,
Written by Himself*, which can be considered both the supreme example and the most characteristic instance of the
slave narrative. Nevertheless, different as it may be in the
brevity of its account of the slave experience, *Behind the Scenes*
resembles Douglass's *Narrative* at several points in its first
three chapters. Among the similarities are Keckley's account
of birth with specifics of place but not date, her description
of the valuation of slaves along with, and in the same manner
as, the valuation of brute animals such as hogs and horses,

and her embittered portrayal of white men fathering children
on slave women—children who were born into slavery and
thus became a part of the slaveholder's wealth. And there is
also the extraordinarily interesting matter of names and the
quoting of documentary witness outside the line of the narrative proper. Douglass goes through a series of nominal
transformations in his *Narrative*—from Frederick Augustus
Washington Bailey (the name given him by his mother) to
Frederick Bailey or plain Fred to Stanley (the name under
which he escaped from slavery) to Frederick Johnson (the
name under which, according to the marriage certificate re-
produced in the text, James W. C. Pennington married him
to his first wife in New York) to, finally, Frederick Douglass. In *Behind the Scenes,* when we are presented with the
maze of documents that eventually produced emancipation
for the author in St. Louis, we find this very revealing com-
plexity of naming in a transfer of ownership:

> Know all men by these presents, that for and in consideration
> of the love and affection we bear towards our sister, Anne P.
> Garland, of St. Louis, Missouri, and for the further consid-
> eration of $5 in hand paid, we hereby sell and convey unto
> her, the said Anne P. Garland, a negro woman called Lizzie,
> and a negro boy, her son, named George; said Lizzie now
> resides at St. Louis, and is a seamstress, known there as Liz-
> zie Garland, the wife of a yellow man named James, and
> called James Keckley; said George is a bright mulatto boy,
> and is known in St. Louis as Garland's George. We warrant
> these two slaves to be slaves for life, but make no represen-
> tations as to age or health.

Indeed, these emancipation documents, like extratextual documentary material in Douglass's *Narrative* and most of the
other slave narratives, are most remarkable in themselves and

warrant closer, more extended attention than can be given them here.

Even as one notes these similarities, however, one must remark some striking differences of tone, structure, and intention between Elizabeth Keckley's book and a narrative such as Douglass's. One example may suffice: Keckley tells the story of an uncle who had twice lost a pair of plough-lines and who, "rather than be punished the way Colonel Burwell punished his servants," committed suicide. Keckley's surprising and taciturn comment is, "Slavery had its dark side as well as its bright side." The reader of Douglass's *Narrative*, or most of the other slave narratives for that matter, will search a long time and in vain for any intimation of slavery's bright side, but the hint of it in Keckley's account merely suggests that *Behind the Scenes* both is and is not what we might understand by the term *slave narrative*. Even when it rather briefly is in that mode, its perspective, from after four years in the White House, determines a very different story from one told by someone who has very recently escaped from slavery—and told entirely in the service of the abolitionist cause. Moreover, while Elizabeth Keckley was writing partly within an abolitionist tradition, she was also writing within, and simultaneously against, a powerful apologetic tradition, by which I mean a tradition of apology for the South and for the slave system on which the South's economy rested and which determined social structures throughout the Southern states. This peculiar blend of opposed intentions— on the one hand, an indictment of the South's slave system, and on the other hand, an alien apologetics—accounts in part for the special nature of the "slave narrative" portion of Keckley's book.

One other feature that makes the book's first three chapters similar to a number of slave narratives (although Douglass's *Narrative* is not notably one of them) is that at the beginning—and later, but in a different way—Elizabeth Keckley adopts many of the conventions of characterization, tone, and dialogue of nineteenth-century sentimental fiction. "As I sit alone in my room the brain is busy," she writes in the first paragraph,

> and a rapidly moving panorama brings scene after scene before me, some pleasant and others sad; and when I thus greet old familiar faces, I often find myself wondering if I am not living the past over again. The visions are so terribly distinct that I almost imagine them to be real. Hour after hour I sit while the scenes are being shifted; and as I gaze upon the panorama of the past, I realize how crowded with incidents my life has been. Every day seems like a romance within itself, and the years grow into ponderous volumes.

Whether Elizabeth Keckley was assisted in writing *Behind the Scenes* by someone experienced in producing novels of romance and sentiment is quite beside the point; what is really relevant is that there was frequently a close tie and a give-and-take relationship between slave narratives and sentimental fiction. We can take as an example the scene in which Keckley tells of the separation of her parents:

> The announcement fell upon the little circle in that rude-log cabin like a thunderbolt. I can remember the scene as if it were but yesterday;—how my father cried out against the cruel separation; his last kiss; his wild straining of my mother to his bosom; the solemn prayer to Heaven; the tears and sobs—the fearful anguish of broken hearts. The last kiss, the last goodby; and he, my father, was gone, gone forever. The shadow eclipsed the sunshine, and love brought despair. The parting was eternal. The cloud had no silver lining, but I

trust that it will be all silver in heaven. We who are crushed to earth with heavy chains, who travel a weary, rugged, thorny road, groping through midnight darkness on earth, earn our right to enjoy the sunshine in the great hereafter. At the grave, at least, we should be permitted to lay our burdens down, that a new world, a world of brightness, may open to us.

Alongside this passage, written out of Elizabeth Keckley's experience and memories of experience, we might place the following passage from *Uncle Tom's Cabin*, in which Harriet Beecher Stowe imagines what such a separation of husband and wife would be like and what the consequences might be thereafter:

As the boat stopped, a black woman came running wildly up the plank, darted into the crowd, flew up to where the slave gang sat, and threw her arms round that unfortunate piece of merchandise before enumerated,—"John, aged thirty," and with sobs and tears bemoaned him as her husband.

But what needs tell the story, told too oft,—every day told,—of heart-strings rent and broken,—the weak broken and torn for the profit and convenience of the strong! It needs not to be told;—every day is telling it,—telling it, too, in the ear of One who is not deaf, though he be long silent.

If one notes similarities between passages like these and if one remarks the presence of certain conventions of sentimental fiction in Keckley's book and in slave narratives generally, one should also observe that the matter is much more complex than a simple cause-and-effect influence of Stowe's book of 1852 upon Keckley's book of 1868. The relationship of the two was in fact one of interwoven and mutual influences. For one thing, Stowe researched her subject by seeking information about the slave's plantation life from Douglass and others and hence was herself writing under the direct influence of the accounts given by slave narratives and narrators. The truth is that the slave narrative and sentimental fiction were interdeterminative of each other, and both were bound up with—and to a considerable degree bound by—social conventions of the time. In this respect, all of Chapter II ("Girlhood and its Sorrows") is deeply interesting and relevant. In it, the sadistic beating of the eighteen-year-old Elizabeth Keckley, at the behest of a "cold, jealous" mistress, by a schoolmaster who evidently derived some sexual pleasure from the flogging is described right against the account of "a white man . . . [who] had base designs" on the girl. "I do not care to dwell upon this subject," Keckley writes, "for it is one that is fraught with pain. Suffice it to say, that he persecuted me for four years, and I—I—became a mother." Reticence of this sort and frequent silences are characteristic of Keckley's narrative, for as she says, "I am not writing altogether the history of myself . . . [and therefore] will confine my story to the most important incidents which I believe influenced the moulding of my character."

Behind the Scenes is thus not altogether a slave narrative and not exactly an autobiography, although it partakes in part of both of these, nor is it a romance or a sentimental novel, even though it reads at times as if it could be so classified. After the first three chapters, the book could best be described as "memoirs"—i.e., the sort of narrative that is grown out of personal experience but that does not focus on the personal element and describes instead external events and figures who occupy some important place in the affairs of the world. As is appropriate in a volume of memoirs, we hear much of Mrs. Lincoln's opinions and emotions and much of Lincoln's weariness and his teasing humor but little of Elizabeth Keckley's feelings or attitudes. In one indicative episode, Keckley gives a good deal of space to the death of Willie Lincoln, which she renders in language that would not be out of place in Dickens or Harriet Beecher Stowe, but only glancingly and as a kind of footnote to Willie Lincoln's death does she reveal that her own only son had been killed in battle. Even this she divulges, however, mostly to give herself the opportunity to pay credit to Mary Todd Lincoln, saying that "the kind womanly letter that Mrs. Lincoln wrote to me when she heard of my bereavement was full of golden words of comfort." It is as if the Lincolns—their speech, their emotions, their actions—were "important," in Keckley's view, in a way that she would never claim for herself or for her own actions and emotions. Yet the decisive fact for this narrative—and the reader must consciously keep this in mind throughout—is that the figures and events of the story, whether about the Lincolns in their private chambers or about the return to Richmond after the fall of the Confederate capital, are all seen through the eyes of a black woman, a seamstress and dressmaker, who is only a few years removed, by her own efforts, from being a "slave for life." Here, too, in this memoiristic portion of the text, we can see many of the conventions of the sentimental novel in play. And given the circumstances, with Elizabeth Keckley privy to intimate conversations in the Jefferson Davis household as well as in the Lincoln White House, how could it be otherwise? This is the very stuff of romance. Indeed, one might see *Behind the Scenes* as the prototype of the Civil War novel with a few important differences from, for example, *Gone with the Wind:* The action takes place not on a Southern plantation but in the nation's capital; the actors are not self-dramatizing heroes and heroines of the South but are the privately seen leaders of the opposed forces in the struggle over national identity; and the drama is viewed and narrated not by someone whose imagination would return to the antebellum South many years after the war but by an ex-slave seamstress and dressmaker who was there—there in the antebellum South, there in the Washington of the Civil War years, and there when the Union forces were at last triumphant.

Elizabeth Keckley does not dwell often or much insist on this element of the drama, but the reader must not forget that the struggle going on beyond the White House and Washington—the history that unfolds itself as romance in the pages of *Behind the Scenes*—was to determine the character and identity of the nation at the time of its second birth. At issue was whether the violent paradox in the phrase from Frederick Douglass's title—*An American Slave* (and it is not insignificant that Keckley recounts how Douglass was first excluded from, then brought into, the reception on the occasion of Lincoln's second inauguration)—whether that violent paradox should continue to be a part of the life of the nation or whether the Emancipation Proclamation should be effectively subjoined to the Declaration of Independence. The question was whether, in Lincoln's words, "this nation shall have a new birth of freedom" that would effectively grant to the black population those rights claimed for all citizens of the emerging nation in the Declaration of Independence. This issue is in a sense the subtext (or one might say, the subsuming national text) of all the slave narratives, even—or perhaps especially—of those published before Lincoln issued the Proclamation. And we must imagine that subtext to be yet more significant and more poignant, because less likely to be heard, when, as in *Behind the Scenes*, the main text is by a black woman.

Behind the Scenes has never been entirely lost from view, but it needs to be restored to our full conscious awareness, for it is a unique book that, even while being one of a kind, still establishes for itself a rightful place in several different traditions crucial to Afro-American history and literature. Something of a slave narrative, something of a novel of sentiment, something of a memoir retailing events and figures of great national moment, *Behind the Scenes* is also—and now, in the present series, can be seen to be—a highly significant contribution to an evolving tradition of primary importance, a tradition of writing by black women who for far too long have been unknown or disregarded in histories of American literature.

BEHIND THE SCENES.

ELIZABETH KECKLEY.

BEHIND THE SCENES.

BY

ELIZABETH KECKLEY,

FORMERLY A SLAVE, BUT MORE RECENTLY MODISTE, AND FRIEND TO MRS.
ABRAHAM LINCOLN.

OR,

THIRTY YEARS A SLAVE, AND FOUR YEARS IN THE WHITE HOUSE.

NEW YORK:
G. W. Carleton & Co., Publishers.
M DCCC LXVIII.

THE NEW YORK PRINTING COMPANY,
81, 83, *and* 85 *Centre Street,*
NEW YORK.

CONTENTS.

PREFACE.

I HAVE often been asked to write my life, as those who
know me know that it has been an eventful one. At last I
have acceded to the importunities of my friends, and
have hastily sketched some of the striking incidents
that go to make up my history. My life, so full of romance, may sound like a dream to the matter-of-fact
reader, nevertheless everything I have written is strictly true; much has been omitted, but nothing has been
exaggerated. In writing as I have done, I am well
aware that I have invited criticism; but before the critic
judges harshly, let my explanation be carefully read
and weighed. If I have portrayed the dark side of
slavery, I also have painted the bright side. The good
that I have said of human servitude should be thrown
into the scales with the evil that I have said of it. I
have kind, true-hearted friends in the South as well as
in the North, and I would not wound those Southern

friends by sweeping condemnation, simply because I was once a slave. They were not so much responsible for the curse under which I was born, as the God of nature and the fathers who framed the Constitution for the United States. The law descended to them, and it was but natural that they should recognize it, since it manifestly was their interest to do so. And yet a wrong was inflicted upon me; a cruel custom deprived me of my liberty, and since I was robbed of my dearest right, I would not have been human had I not rebelled against the robbery. God rules the Universe. I was a feeble instrument in His hands, and through me and the enslaved millions of my race, one of the problems was solved that belongs to the great problem of human destiny; and the solution was developed so gradually that there was no great convulsion of the harmonies of natural laws. A solemn truth was thrown to the surface, and what is better still, it was recognized *as a truth* by those who give force to moral laws. An act may be wrong, but unless the ruling power recognizes the wrong, it is useless to hope for a correction of it. Principles may be right, but they are not established within an hour. The masses are slow to reason, and each principle, to acquire moral force, must come to us from the fire of the crucible; the fire may inflict unjust punishment, but then it purifies and renders stronger the principle, not in itself, but in the eyes of those who arrogate judgment to themselves. When the war of the Revolution established the independence of the

American colonies, an evil was perpetuated, slavery was more firmly established; and since the evil had been planted, it must pass through certain stages before it could be eradicated. In fact, we give but little thought to the plant of evil until it grows to such monstrous proportions that it overshadows important interests; then the efforts to destroy it become earnest. As one of the victims of slavery I drank of the bitter water; but then, since destiny willed it so, and since I aided in bringing a solemn truth to the surface *as a truth*, perhaps I have no right to complain. Here, as in all things pertaining to life, I can afford to be charitable.

It may be charged that I have written too freely on some questions, especially in regard to Mrs. Lincoln. I do not think so; at least I have been prompted by the purest motive. Mrs. Lincoln, by her own acts, forced herself into notoriety. She stepped beyond the formal lines which hedge about a private life, and invited public criticism. The people have judged her harshly, and no woman was ever more traduced in the public prints of the country. The people knew nothing of the secret history of her transactions, therefore they judged her by what was thrown to the surface. For an act may be wrong judged purely by itself, but when the motive that prompted the act is understood, it is construed differently. I lay it down as an axiom, that only that is criminal in the sight of God where crime is meditated. Mrs. Lincoln may have been imprudent, but since her intentions were good, she should be judged more kindly than she has been. But the world do not know what her intentions were; they have only been made acquainted with her acts without knowing what feeling guided her actions. If the world are to judge her as I have judged her, they must be introduced to the secret history of her transactions. The veil of mystery must be drawn aside; the origin of a fact must be brought to light with the naked fact itself. If I have betrayed confidence in anything I have published, it has been to place Mrs. Lincoln in a better light before the world. A breach of trust—if breach it can be called—of this kind is always excusable. My own character, as well as the character of Mrs. Lincoln, is at stake, since I have been intimately associated with that lady in the most eventful periods of her life. I have been her confidante, and if evil charges are laid at her door, they also must be laid at mine, since I have been a party to all her movements. To defend myself I must defend the lady that I have served. The world have judged Mrs. Lincoln by the facts which float upon the surface, and through her have partially judged me, and the only way to convince them that wrong was not meditated is to explain the motives that actuated us. I have written nothing that can place Mrs. Lincoln in a worse light before the world than the light in which she now stands, therefore the secret history that I publish can do her no harm. I have excluded everything of a personal character from her letters; the extracts introduced only

refer to public men, and are such as to throw light
upon her unfortunate adventure in New York. These
letters were not written for publication, for which
reason they are all the more valuable; they are the
frank overflowings of the heart, the outcropping of im-
pulse, the key to genuine motives. They prove the
motive to have been pure, and if they shall help to stifle
the voice of calumny, I am content. I do not forget,
before the public journals vilified Mrs. Lincoln, that ladies
who moved in the Washington circle in which she
moved, freely canvassed her character among themselves. They gloated over many a tale of scandal that
grew out of gossip in their own circle. If these ladies
could say everything bad of the wife of the President,
why should I not be permitted to lay her secret history
bare, especially when that history plainly shows that her
life, like all lives, has its good side as well as its bad
side ? None of us are perfect, for which reason we
should heed the voice of charity when it whispers
in our ears, "Do not magnify the imperfections of
others." Had Mrs. Lincoln's acts never become public property, I should not have published to the world
the secret chapters of her life. I am not the special
champion of the widow of our lamented President; the
reader of the pages which follow will discover that I
have written with the utmost frankness in regard to her
—have exposed her faults as well as given her credit for
honest motives. I wish the world to judge her as she
is, free from the exaggerations of praise or scandal, since

I have been associated with her in so many things that have provoked hostile criticism; and the judgment that the world may pass upon her, I flatter myself, will present my own actions in a better light.

ELIZABETH KECKLEY.

14 CARROLL PLACE, NEW YORK, March 14, 1868.

ßEHIND THE ßCENES.

CHAPTER I.

WHERE I WAS BORN.

Y life has been an eventful one. I was born a slave—was the child of slave parents—therefore I came upon the earth free in God-like thought, but fettered in action. My birthplace was Dinwiddie Court-House, in Virginia. My recollections of childhood are distinct, perhaps for the reason that many stirring incidents are associated with that period. I am now on the shady side of forty, and as I sit alone in my room the brain is busy, and a rapidly moving panorama brings scene after scene before me, some pleasant and others sad; and when I thus greet old familiar faces, I often find myself wondering if I am not living the past over again. The visions are so terribly distinct that I almost imagine them to be real. Hour after hour I sit while the scenes are being shifted; and as I gaze upon the panorama of the past, I realize how crowded with incidents my life has been. Every day seems like a romance within itself, and the years grow into ponderous volumes. As I cannot condense, I must omit many strange passages in my history. From such a wilderness of events it is difficult to make a selection, but as I am not writing altogether the history of myself, I will confine my story to the most important incidents which I believe influenced the moulding of my character. As I glance over the crowded sea of the past, these incidents stand forth prominently, the guide-posts of memory. I presume that I must have been four years old when I first began to remember; at least, I cannot now recall anything occurring previous to this period. My master, Col. A. Burwell, was somewhat unsettled in his business affairs, and while I was yet an infant he made several removals. While living at Hampton Sidney College, Prince Edward County, Va., Mrs. Burwell gave birth to a daughter, a sweet, black-eyed baby, my earliest and fondest pet. To take care of this baby was my first duty. True, I was but a child myself—only four years old—but then I had been raised in a hardy school—had been taught to rely upon myself, and to prepare myself to render assistance to others. The lesson was not a bitter one, for I was too young to indulge in philosophy, and the precepts that I then treasured and practised I believe developed those principles of character which have enabled me to triumph over so many difficulties. Notwithstanding all the wrongs that slavery heaped upon me, I can bless it for one thing—youth's important lesson of self-reliance. The baby was named Elizabeth, and it was pleasant to me to be assigned a duty in connection with it, for the discharge of that duty transferred me from the rude cabin to the household of my master. My simple attire was a short dress and a little white apron. My old mistress encouraged me in rocking the cradle, by telling me that if I would watch over the baby well, keep the flies out of its face, and not let it cry, I should be its little maid. This was a golden promise, and I required no better inducement for the faithful performance of my task. I began to rock the cradle most industriously, when lo! out pitched little pet on the floor. I instantly cried out, "Oh! the baby is on the floor;" and, not knowing what to do, I seized the fire-shovel in my perplexity, and was trying to shovel up my tender charge, when my mistress called to me to let the child alone, and then ordered that I be taken out and lashed for my carelessness.

The blows were not administered with a light
hand, I assure you, and doubtless the severity
of the lashing has made me remember the incident so well. This was the first time I was
punished in this cruel way, but not the last.
The black-eyed baby that I called my pet grew
into a self-willed girl, and in after years was
the cause of much trouble to me. I grew strong
and healthy, and, notwithstanding I knit socks
and attended to various kinds of work, I was
repeatedly told, when even fourteen years old,
that I would never be worth my salt. When
I was eight, Mr. Burwell's family consisted of
six sons and four daughters, with a large family
of servants. My mother was kind and forbear-
ing; Mrs. Burwell a hard task-master; and as
mother had so much work to do in making
clothes, etc., for the family, besides the slaves, I
determined to render her all the assistance in
my power, and in rendering her such assistance
my young energies were taxed to the utmost

I was my mother's only child, which made her love for me all the stronger. I did not know much of my father, for he was the slave of another man, and when Mr. Burwell moved from Dinwiddie he was separated from us, and only allowed to visit my mother twice a year—during the Easter holidays and Christmas. At last Mr. Burwell determined to reward my mother, by making an arrangement with the owner of my father, by which the separation of my parents could be brought to an end. It was a bright day, indeed, for my mother when it was announced that my father was coming to live with us. The old weary look faded from her face, and she worked as if her heart was in every task. But the golden days did not last long. The radiant dream faded all too soon.

In the morning my father called me to him and kissed me, then held me out at arms' length as if he were regarding his child with pride. "She is growing into a large fine girl," he remarked to my mother. "I dun no which I like best, you or Lizzie, as both are so dear to me." My mother's name was Agnes, and my father delighted to call me his "Little Lizzie." While yet my father and mother were speaking hopefully, joyfully of the future, Mr. Burwell came to the cabin, with a letter in his hand. He was a kind master in some things, and as gently as possible informed my parents that they must part; for in two hours my father must join his master at Dinwiddie, and go with him to the West, where he had determined to make his future home. The announcement fell upon the little circle in that rude-log cabin like a thunderbolt. I can remember the scene as if it were but yesterday;—how my father cried out against the cruel separation; his last kiss; his wild straining of my mother to his bosom; the solemn prayer to Heaven; the tears and sobs—the fearful anguish of broken hearts. The last kiss, the last goodby; and he, my father, was gone, gone forever.

The shadow eclipsed the sunshine, and love brought despair. The parting was eternal. The cloud had no silver lining, but I trust that it will be all silver in heaven. We who are crushed to earth with heavy chains, who travel a weary, rugged, thorny road, groping through midnight darkness on earth, earn our right to enjoy the sunshine in the great hereafter. At the grave, at least, we should be permitted to lay our burdens down, that a new world, a world of brightness, may open to us. The light that is denied us here should grow into a flood of effulgence beyond the dark, mysterious shadows of death. Deep as was the distress of my mother in parting with my father, her sorrow did not screen her from insult. My old mistress said to her: "Stop your nonsense; there is no necessity for you putting on airs. Your husband is not the only slave that has been sold from his family, and you are not the only one that has had to part. There are plenty more men about here, and if you want a husband so badly, stop your crying and go and find another." To these unfeeling words my mother made no reply. She turned away in stoical silence, with a curl of that loathing scorn upon her lips which swelled in her heart.

My father and mother never met again in this world. They kept up a regular correspondence for years, and the most precious mementoes of my existence are the faded old letters that he wrote, full of love, and always hoping that the future would bring brighter days. In nearly every letter is a message for me. " Tell my darling little Lizzie," he writes, " to be a good girl, and to learn her book. Kiss her for me, and tell her that I will come to see her some day." Thus he wrote time and again, but he never came. He lived in hope, but died without ever seeing his wife and child.

I note a few extracts from one of my father's letters to my mother, following copy literally:

2

" Shelbyville, Sept. 6, 1833.

" Mrs. Agnes Hobbs.

" Dear Wife : My dear biloved wife I am more
than glad to meet with opportunty writce thes
few lines to you by my Mistress who ar now
about starterng to virginia, and sevl others of my
old friends are with her ; in compeney Mrs. Ann
Rus the wife of master Thos Rus and Dan Wood-
iard and his family and I am very sorry that I
havn the chance to go with them as I feele
Determid to see you If life last again. I am now
here and out at this pleace so I am not abble to
get of at this time. I am write well and hearty
and all the rest of masters family. I heard this
eveng by Mistress that ar just from theree all
sends love to you and all my old frends. I am
a living in a town called Shelbyville and I have
wrote a greate many letters since Ive beene here
and almost been reeady to my selfe that its out
of the question to write any more at tall : my dear
wife I dont feeld no whys like giving out writing

to you as yet and I hope when you get this letter
that you be Inncougege to write me a letter.   I
am well satisfied at my living at this place I am a
making money for my own benifit and I hope
that its to yours also If I live to see Nexct year
I shall heve my own time from master by giving
him 100 and twenty Dollars a year and I thinke I
shall be doing good bisness at that and heve something more thean all that.   I hope with gods
helpe that I may be abble to rejoys with you on
the earth and In heaven lets meet when will I am
detemnid to nuver stope praying, not in this earth
and I hope to praise god In glory there weel
meet to part no more forever.   So my dear wife
I hope to meet you In paradase to prase god forever * * * * * I want Elizabeth to be a good
girl and not to thinke that becasue I am bound so
fare that gods not abble to open the way * * * *

"GEORGE PLEASANT,

"*Hobbs a servant of Grum.*"

The last letter that my mother received from my

father was dated Shelbyville, Tennessee, March
20, 1839. He writes in a cheerful strain, and
hopes to see her soon. Alas! he looked forward
to a meeting in vain. Year after year the one
great hope swelled in his heart, but the hope was
only realized beyond the dark portals of the grave.

When I was about seven years old I witnessed,
for the first time, the sale of a human being.
We were living at Prince Edward, in Virginia,
and master had just purchased his hogs for the
winter, for which he was unable to pay in full.
To escape from his embarrassment it was necessary to sell one of the slaves. Little Joe, the son
of the cook, was selected as the victim. His
mother was ordered to dress him up in his Sunday clothes, and send him to the house. He
came in with a bright face, was placed in the
scales, and was sold, like the hogs, at so much
per pound. His mother was kept in ignorance
of the transaction, but her suspicions were
aroused. When her son started for Petersburgh
in the wagon, the truth began to dawn upon her

mind, and she pleaded piteously that her boy should not be taken from her; but master quieted her by telling her that he was simply going to town with the wagon, and would be back in the morning. Morning came, but little Joe did not return to his mother. Morning after morning passed, and the mother went down to the grave without ever seeing her child again. One day she was whipped for grieving for her lost boy. Colonel Burwell never liked to see one of his slaves wear a sorrowful face, and those who offended in this particular way were always punished. Alas! the sunny face of the slave is not always an indication of sunshine in the heart. Colonel Burwell at one time owned about seventy slaves, all of which were sold, and in a majority of instances wives were separated from husbands and children from their parents. Slavery in the Border States forty years ago was different from what it was twenty years ago. Time seemed to soften the hearts of master and mistress, and to insure kinder and more humane treatment to bondsmen and bondswomen. When I was quite a child, an incident occurred which my mother afterward impressed more strongly on my mind. One of my uncles, a slave of Colonel Burwell, lost a pair of plough-lines, and when the loss was made known the master gave him a new pair, and told him that if he did not take care of them he would punish him severely. In a few weeks the second pair of lines was stolen, and my uncle hung himself rather than meet the displeasure of his master. My mother went to the spring in the morning for a pail of water, and on looking up into the willow tree which shaded the bubbling crystal stream, she discovered the lifeless form of her brother suspended beneath one of the strong branches. Rather than be punished the way Colonel Burwell punished his servants, he took his own life. Slavery had its dark side as well as its bright side.

CHAPTER II.

GIRLHOOD AND ITS SORROWS.

 MUST pass rapidly over the stirring events of my early life. When I was about fourteen years old I went to live with my master's eldest son, a Presbyterian minister. His salary was small, and he was burdened with a helpless wife, a girl that he had married in the humble walks of life. She was morbidly sensitive, and imagined that I regarded her with contemptuous feelings because she was of poor parentage. I was their only servant, and a gracious loan at that. They were not able to buy me, so my old master sought to render them assistance by allowing them the benefit of my services. From the very first I did the work of three servants, and yet I was scolded and regarded with distrust. The years passed slowly, and I continued to serve them, and at the same time grew into strong, healthy womanhood. I was nearly eighteen when we removed from Virginia to Hillsboro', North Carolina, where young Mr. Burwell took charge of a church. The salary was small, and we still had to practise the closest economy. Mr. Bingham, a hard, cruel man, the village schoolmaster, was a member of my young master's church, and he was a frequent visitor to the parsonage. She whom I called mistress seemed to be desirous to wreak vengeance on me for something, and Bingham became her ready tool. During this time my master was unusually kind to me; he was naturally a good-hearted man, but was influenced by his wife. It was Saturday evening, and while I was bending over the bed, watching the baby that I had just hushed into slumber, Mr. Bingham came to the door and asked me to go with him to his study. Wondering what he meant by his strange request, I followed him, and when we had entered the study he closed the door, and in his blunt way remarked: "Lizzie, I am going to flog you." I was thunderstruck, and tried to think if I had been remiss in anything. I could not recollect of doing anything to deserve punishment, and with surprise exclaimed: "Whip me, Mr. Bingham! what for?"

"No matter," he replied, "I am going to whip you, so take down your dress this instant."

Recollect, I was eighteen years of age, was a woman fully developed, and yet this man coolly bade me take down my dress. I drew myself up proudly, firmly, and said: "No, Mr. Bingham, I shall not take down my dress before you. Moreover, you shall not whip me unless you prove the stronger. Nobody has a right to whip me but my own master, and nobody shall do so if I can prevent it."

2*

My words seemed to exasperate him. He seized a rope, caught me roughly, and tried to tie me. I resisted with all my strength, but he was the stronger of the two, and after a hard struggle succeeded in binding my hands and tearing my dress from my back. Then he picked up a rawhide, and began to ply it freely over my shoulders. With steady hand and practised eye he would raise the instrument of torture, nerve himself for a blow, and with fearful force the rawhide descended upon the quivering flesh. It cut the skin, raised great welts, and the warm blood trickled down my back. Oh God! I can feel the torture now—the terrible, excruciating agony of those moments. I did not scream; I was too proud to let my tormentor know what I was suffering. I closed my lips firmly, that not even a groan might escape from them, and I stood like a statue while the keen lash cut deep into my flesh. As soon as I was released, stunned with pain, bruised and bleeding, I went home and rushed into the presence of the pastor and his wife, wildly exclaiming : " Master Robert, why did you let Mr. Bingham flog me ? What have I done that I should be so punished ? "

" Go away," he gruffly answered, " do not bother me."

I would not be put off thus. " What *have* I done ? I *will* know why I have been flogged."

I saw his cheeks flush with anger, but I did not move. He rose to his feet, and on my refusing to go without an explanation, seized a chair, struck me, and felled me to the floor. I rose, bewildered, almost dead with pain, crept to my room, dressed my bruised arms and back as best I could, and then lay down, but not to sleep. No, I could not sleep, for I was suffering mental as well as bodily torture. My spirit rebelled against the unjustness that had been inflicted upon me, and though I tried to smother my anger and to forgive those who had been so cruel to me, it was impossible. The next morning I was more

calm, and I believe that I could then have for
given everything for the sake of one kind word.
But the kind word was not proffered, and it
may be possible that I grew somewhat wayward
and sullen. Though I had faults, I know now,
as I felt then, harshness was the poorest inducement for the correction of them. It seems that
Mr. Bingham had pledged himself to Mrs. Burwell to subdue what he called my "stubborn
pride." On Friday following the Saturday on
which I was so savagely beaten, Mr. Bingham
again directed me to come to his study. I
went, but with the determination to offer resistance should he attempt to flog me again.
On entering the room I found him prepared with
a new rope and a new cowhide. I told him
that I was ready to die, but that he could not
conquer me. In struggling with him I bit his
finger severely, when he seized a heavy stick and
beat me with it in a shameful manner. Again
I went home sore and bleeding, but with pride as

strong and defiant as ever. The following Thursday Mr. Bingham again tried to conquer me, but in vain. We struggled, and he struck me many savage blows. As I stood bleeding before him, nearly exhausted with his efforts, he burst into tears, and declared that it would be a sin to beat me any more. My suffering at last subdued his hard heart; he asked my forgiveness, and afterwards was an altered man. He was never known to strike one of his servants from that day forward. Mr. Burwell, he who preached the love of Heaven, who glorified the precepts and examples of Christ, who expounded the Holy Scriptures Sabbath after Sabbath from the pulpit, when Mr. Bingham refused to whip me any more, was urged by his wife to punish me himself. One morning he went to the wood-pile, took an oak broom, cut the handle off, and with this heavy handle attempted to conquer me. I fought him, but he proved the strongest. At the sight of my bleeding form, his wife fell upon her knees and begged him to desist. My distress even touched her cold, jealous heart. I was so badly bruised that I was unable to leave my bed for five days. I will not dwell upon the bitter anguish of these hours, for even the thought of them now makes me shudder. The Rev. Mr. Burwell was not yet satisfied. He resolved to make another attempt to subdue my proud, rebellious spirit—made the attempt and again failed, when he told me, with an air of penitence, that he should never strike me another blow; and faithfully he kept his word. These revolting scenes created a great sensation at the time, were the talk of the town and neighborhood, and I flatter myself that the actions of those who had conspired against me were not viewed in a light to reflect much credit upon them.

The savage efforts to subdue my pride were not the only things that brought me suffering and deep mortification during my residence at Hillsboro'. I was regarded as fair-looking for

one of my race, and for four years a white man—
I spare the world his name—had base designs
upon me. I do not care to dwell upon this subject, for it is one that is fraught with pain.
Suffice it to say, that he persecuted me for four
years, and I—I—became a mother. The child
of which he was the father was the only child
that I ever brought into the world. If my poor
boy ever suffered any humiliating pangs on account of birth, he could not blame his mother,
for God knows that she did not wish to give
him life; he must blame the edicts of that society which deemed it no crime to undermine
the virtue of girls in my then position.

Among the old letters preserved by my mother
I find the following, written by myself while
at Hillsboro'. In this connection I desire to
state that Rev. Robert Burwell is now living * at
Charlotte, North Carolina:—

"Hillsboro', April 10, 1838.
"My Dear Mother:—I have been intending
* March, 1868.

to write to you for a long time, but numerous things have prevented, and for that reason you must excuse me.

"I thought very hard of you for not writing to me, but hope that you will answer this letter as soon as you receive it, and tell me how you like Marsfield, and if you have seen any of my old acquaintances, or if you yet know any of the brick-house people who I think so much of. I want to hear of the family at home very much, indeed. I really believe you and all the family have forgotten me, if not I certainly should have heard from some of you since you left Boyton, if it was only a line ; nevertheless I love you all very dearly, and shall, although I may never see you again, nor do I ever expect to. Miss Anna is going to Petersburgh next winter, but she says that she does not intend to take me ; what reason she has for leaving me I cannot tell. I have often wished that I lived where I knew I never could see you, for then I would not have my hopes raised, and to be disappointed in this manner; however, it is said that a bad beginning makes a good ending, but I hardly expect to see that happy day at this place. Give my love to all the family, both white and black. I was very much obliged to you for the presents you sent me last summer, though it is quite late in the day to be thanking for them. Tell Aunt Bella that I was very much obliged to her for her present; I have been so particular with it that I have only worn it once.

" There have been six weddings since October; the most respectable one was about a fortnight ago; I was asked to be the first attendant, but, as usual with all my expectations, I was disappointed, for on the wedding-day I felt more like being locked up in a three-cornered box than attending a wedding. About a week before Christmas I was bridesmaid for Ann Nash; when the night came I was in quite a trouble;

I did not know whether my frock was clean or
dirty ; I only had a week's notice, and the body
and sleeves to make, and only one hour every
night to work on it, so you can see with, these
troubles to overcome my chance was rather slim.
I must now close, although I could fill ten pages
with my griefs and misfortunes; no tongue could
express them as I feel ; don't forget me though ;
and answer my letters soon. I will write you
again, and would write more now, but Miss Anna
says it is time I had finished.   Tell Miss
Elizabeth that I wish she would make haste and
get married, for mistress says that I belong to her
when she gets married.

"I wish you would send me a pretty frock this
summer; if you will send it to Mrs. Robertson's
Miss Bet will send it to me.

"Farewell, darling mother.

"Your affectionate daughter,

"Elizabeth Hobbs."

CHAPTER III.

How I Gained my Freedom.

HE years passed and brought many changes to me, but on these I will not dwell, as I wish to hasten to the most interesting part of my story. My troubles in North Carolina were brought to an end by my unexpected return to Virginia, where I lived with Mr. Garland, who had married Miss Ann Burwell, one of my old master's daughters. His life was not a prosperous one, and after struggling with the world for several years he left his native State, a disappointed man. He moved to St. Louis, hoping to improve his fortune in the West;

but ill luck followed him there, and he seemed to be unable to escape from the influence of the evil star of his destiny. When his family, myself included, joined him in his new home on the banks of the Mississippi, we found him so poor that he was unable to pay the dues on a letter advertised as in the post-office for him. The necessities of the family were so great, that it was proposed to place my mother out at service. The idea was shocking to me. Every gray hair in her old head was dear to me, and I could not bear the thought of her going to work for strangers. She had been raised in the family, had watched the growth of each child from infancy to maturity; they had been the objects of her kindest care, and she was wound round about them as the vine winds itself about the rugged oak. They had been the central figures in her dream of life—a dream beautiful to her, since she had basked in the sunshine of no other. And now they proposed to destroy each tendril of affection, to cloud the sunshine of her existence when the day was drawing to a close, when the shadows of solemn night were rapidly approaching. My mother, my poor aged mother, go among strangers to toil for a living! No, a thousand times no! I would rather work my fingers to the bone, bend over my sewing till the film of blindness gathered in my eyes; nay, even beg from street to street. I told Mr. Garland so, and he gave me permission to see what I could do. I was fortunate in obtaining work, and in a short time I had acquired something of a reputation as a seamstress and dress-maker. The best ladies in St. Louis were my patrons, and when my reputation was once established I never lacked for orders. With my needle I kept bread in the mouths of seventeen persons for two years and five months. While I was working so hard that others might live in comparative comfort, and move in those circles of society to which their birth gave them entrance, the thought often

occurred to me whether I was really worth my
salt or not; and then perhaps the lips curled
with a bitter sneer. It may seem strange that
I should place so much emphasis upon words
thoughtlessly, idly spoken; but then we do many
strange things in life, and cannot always explain
the motives that actuate us. The heavy task
was too much for me, and my health began to
give way. About this time Mr. Keckley, whom
I had met in Virginia, and learned to regard
with more than friendship, came to St. Louis.
He sought my hand in marriage, and for a long
time I refused to consider his proposal; for I
could not bear the thought of bringing children
into slavery—of adding one single recruit to the
millions bound to hopeless servitude, fettered
and shackled with chains stronger and heavier
than manacles of iron. I made a proposition to
buy myself and son; the proposition was bluntly
declined, and I was commanded never to broach
the subject again. I would not be put off thus,

for hope pointed to a freer, brighter life in the future. Why should my son be held in slavery? I often asked myself. He came into the world through no will of mine, and yet, God only knows how I loved him. The Anglo-Saxon blood as well as the African flowed in his veins; the two currents commingled—one singing of freedom, the other silent and sullen with generations of despair. Why should not the Anglo-Saxon triumpn—why should it be weighed down with the rich blood typical of the tropics? Must the life-current of one race bind the other race in chains as strong and enduring as if there had been no Anglo-Saxon taint? By the laws of God and nature, as interpreted by man, one-half of my boy was free, and why should not this fair birthright of freedom remove the curse from the other half—raise it into the bright, joyous sunshine of liberty? I could not answer these questions of my heart that almost maddened me, and I learned to regard human philosophy with dis-

trust. Much as I respected the authority of my
master, I could not remain silent on a subject
that so nearly concerned me. One day, when I
insisted on knowing whether he would permit
me to purchase myself, and what price I must
pay for myself, he turned to me in a petulant
manner, thrust his hand into his pocket, drew
forth a bright silver quarter of a dollar, and proffering it to me, said:

"Lizzie, I have told you often not to trouble
me with such a question. If you really wish to
leave me, take this: it will pay the passage of
yourself and boy on the ferry-boat, and when you
are on the other side of the river you will be
free. It is the cheapest way that I know of to
accomplish what you desire."

I looked at him in astonishment, and earnestly
replied: "No, master, I do not wish to be free
in such a manner. If such had been my wish, I
should never have troubled you about obtaining
your consent to my purchasing myself. I can

cross the river any day, as you well know, and have frequently done so, but will never leave you in such a manner. By the laws of the land I am your slave—you are my master, and I will only be free by such means as the laws of the country provide." He expected this answer, and I knew that he was pleased. Some time afterwards he told me that he had reconsidered the question; that I had served his family faithfully; that I deserved my freedom, and that he would take $1200 for myself and boy.

This was joyful intelligence for me, and the reflection of hope gave a silver lining to the dark cloud of my life—faint, it is true, but still a silver lining.

Taking a prospective glance at liberty, I consented to marry. The wedding was a great event in the family. The ceremony took place in the parlor, in the presence of the family and a number of guests. Mr. Garland gave me away, and the pastor, Bishop Hawks, performed the

3

ceremony, who had solemnized the bridals of Mr.
G.'s own children. The day was a happy one,
but it faded all too soon. Mr. Keckley—let me
speak kindly of his faults—proved dissipated, and
a burden instead of a helpmate. More than all,
I learned that he was a slave instead of a free
man, as he represented himself to be. With the
simple explanation that I lived with him eight
years, let charity draw around him the mantle of
silence.

I went to work in earnest to purchase my
freedom, but the years passed, and I was still a
slave. Mr. Garland's family claimed so much of
my attention—in fact, I supported them—that I
was not able to accumulate anything. In the
mean time Mr. Garland died, and Mr. Burwell, a
Mississippi planter, came to St. Louis to settle
up the estate. He was a kind-hearted man, and
said I should be free, and would afford me every
facility to raise the necessary amount to pay the
price of my liberty. Several schemes were urged

upon me by my friends. At last I formed a resolution to go to New York, state my case, and appeal to the benevolence of the people. The plan seemed feasible, and I made preparations to carry it out. When I was almost ready to turn my face northward, Mrs. Garland told me that she would require the names of six gentlemen who would vouch for my return, and become responsible for the amount at which I was valued. I had many friends in St. Louis, and as I believed that they had confidence in me, I felt that I could readily obtain the names desired. I started out, stated my case, and obtained five signatures to the paper, and my heart throbbed with pleasure, for I did not believe that the sixth would refuse me. I called, he listened patiently, then remarked:

"Yes, yes, Lizzie; the scheme is a fair one, and you shall have my name. But I shall bid you good-by when you start."

"Good-by for a short time," I ventured to add.

"No, good-by for all time," and he looked at me as if he would read my very soul with his eyes.

I was startled. "What do you mean, Mr. Farrow? Surely you do not think that I do not mean to come back?"

"No."

"No, what then?"

"Simply this: you *mean* to come back, that is, you *mean* so *now*, but you never will. When you reach New York the abolitionists will tell you what savages we are, and they will prevail on you to stay there; and we shall never see you again."

"'But I assure you, Mr. Farrow, you are mistaken. I not only *mean* to come back, but *will* come back, and pay every cent of the twelve hundred dollars for myself and child."

I was beginning to feel sick at heart, for I could not accept the signature of this man when he had no faith in my pledges. No; slavery, eternal slavery rather than be regarded with distrust by those whose respect I esteemed.

"But—I am not mistaken," he persisted. "Time will show. When you start for the North I shall bid you good-by."

The heart grew heavy. Every ray of sunshine was eclipsed. With humbled pride, weary step, tearful face, and a dull, aching pain, I left the house. I walked along the street mechanically. The cloud had no silver lining now. The rose-buds of hope had withered and died without lifting up their heads to receive the dew kiss of morning. There was no morning for me—all was night, dark night.

I reached my own home, and weeping threw myself upon the bed. My trunk was packed, my luncheon was prepared by mother, the cars were ready to bear me where I would not hear the clank of chains, where I would breathe the free, invigorating breezes of the glorious North. I had dreamed such a happy dream, in imagination had drunk of the water, the pure, sweet crystal water of life, but now—now—the flowers had withered before my eyes; darkness had settled down upon me like a pall, and I was left alone with cruel mocking shadows.

The first paroxysm of grief was scarcely over, when a carriage stopped in front of the house; Mrs. Le Bourgois, one of my kind patrons, got out of it and entered the door. She seemed to bring sunshine with her handsome cheery face. She came to where I was, and in her sweet way said:—

"Lizzie, I hear that you are going to New York to beg for money to buy your freedom. I have been thinking over the matter, and told Ma it would be a shame to allow you to go North to *beg* for what we should *give* you. You have many friends in St. Louis, and I am going to raise the twelve hundred dollars required among them. I have two hundred dollars put away for a present; am indebted to you one hundred dol lars; mother owes you fifty dollars, and will add another fifty to it; and as I do not want the present, I will make the money a present to you. Don't start for New York now until I see what I can do among your friends."

Like a ray of sunshine she came, and like a ray of sunshine she went away. The flowers no longer were withered, drooping. Again they seemed to bud and grow in fragrance and beauty. Mrs. Le Bourgois, God bless her dear good heart, was more than successful. The twelve hundred dollars were raised, and at last my son and myself were free. Free, free! what a glorious ring to the word. Free! the bitter heart-struggle was over. Free! the soul could go out to heaven and to God with no chains to clog its flight or pull it down. Free! the earth wore a brighter look, and the very stars seemed to sing with joy. Yes, free! free by the laws of man and the smile of God—and Heaven bless them who made me so!

The following, copied from the original papers, contain, in brief, the history of my emancipation :—

" I promise to give Lizzie and her son George their freedom, on the payment of $1200.

" ANNE P. GARLAND.

" June 27, 1855."

" LIZZY :—I send you this note to sign for the sum of $75, and when I give you the whole amount you will then sign the other note for $100.

"ELLEN M. DOAN.

" In the paper you will find $25 ; see it is all right before the girl leaves."

" I have received of Lizzy Keckley $950, which I have deposited with Darby & Barksdale for her—$600 on the 21st July, $300 on the 27th and 28th of July, and $50 on 13th August, 1855.

" I have and shall make use of said money for Lizzy's benefit, and hereby guarantee to her one per cent. per month—as much more as can be made she shall have. The one per cent., as it may be checked out, I will be responsible for myself, as well as for the whole amount, when it shall be needed by her.

"WILLIS L. WILLIAMS.

"ST. LOUIS, 13th August, 1855."

"Know all men by these presents, that for and in consideration of the love and affection we bear towards our sister, Anne P. Garland, of St. Louis, Missouri, and for the further consideration of $5 in hand paid, we hereby sell and convey unto her, the said Anne P. Garland, a negro woman named Lizzie, and a negro boy, her son, named George; said Lizzie now resides at St. Louis, and is a seamstress, known there as Lizzie Garland, the wife of a yellow man named James, and called James Keckley; said George is a bright mulatto boy, and is known in St. Louis as Garland's George. We warrant these two slaves to be slaves for life, but make no representations as to age or health.

"Witness our hands and seals, this 10th day of August, 1855.

"JAS. R. PUTNAM, [L.S.]

"E. M. PUTNAM, [L.S.]

"A. BURWELL, [L.S.]"

"The State of Mississipi, Warren
County, City of Vicksburg. } *ss.*

"Be it remembered, that on the tenth day of August, in the year of our Lord one thousand eight hundred and fifty-five, before me, Francis N. Steele, a Commissioner, resident in the city of Vicksburg, duly commissioned and qualified by the executive authority, and under the laws of the State of Missouri, to take the acknowledgment of deeds, etc., to be used or recorded therein, personally appeared James R. Putnam and E. M. Putnam, his wife, and Armistead Burwell, to me known to be the individuals named in, and who executed the foregoing conveyance, and acknowledged that they executed the same for the purposes therein mentioned ; and the E. M Putnam being by me examined apart from her husband, and being fully acquainted with the contents of the foregoing conveyance, acknowledged that she executed the same freely, and relinquished her dower, and any other claim she might have in and to the property therein mentioned, freely, and without fear, compulsion, or undue influence of her said husband.

"In witness whereof I have hereunto set my hand and affixed my official seal, this 10th day of August, A.D. 1855.

[L.S.] "F. N. STEELE,
" *Commissioner for Missouri.*"

"Know all men that I, Anne P. Garland, of the County and City of St. Louis, State of Missouri, for and in consideration of the sum of $1200, to me in hand paid this day in cash, hereby eman-

cipate my negro woman Lizzie, and her son
George; the said Lizzie is known in St. Louis
as the wife of James, who is called James
Keckley; is of light complexion, about 37 years
of age, by trade a dress-maker, and called by
those who know her Garland's Lizzie.   The
said boy, George, is the only child of Lizzie,
is about 16 years of age, and is almost white,
and called by those who know him Garland's
George.

"Witness my hand and seal, this 13th day of
November, 1855.

                    " ANNE P. GARLAND, [L.S.]

    "Witness:—JOHN WICKHAM,

          " WILLIS L. WILLIAMS."

In St. Louis Circuit Court, October Term, 1855.
November 15, 1855.

        " State of Missouri, ⎫ *ss.*
        County of St. Louis. ⎭

    "Be it remembered, that on this fifteenth day of
November, eighteen hundred and fifty-five, in

open court came John Wickham and Willis L. Williams, these two subscribing witnesses, examined under oath to that effect, proved the execution and acknowledgment of said deed by Anne P. Garland to Lizzie and her son George, which said proof of acknowledgment is entered on the record of the court of that day.

"In testimony whereof I hereto set my hand and affix the seal of said court, at office in the City of St. Louis, the day and year last aforesaid.

[L.S.] "WM. J. HAMMOND, *Clerk.*"

"State of Missouri, } *ss.*
County of St. Louis. }

"I, Wm. J. Hammond, Clerk of the Circuit Court within and for the county aforesaid, certify the foregoing to be a true copy of a deed of emancipation from Anne P. Garland to Lizzie and her son George, as fully as the same remain in my office.

"In testimony whereof I hereto set my hand and

affix the seal of said court, at office in the City of St. Louis, this fifteenth day of November, 1855.

"WM. J. HAMMOND, *Clerk.*
"By WM. A. PENNINGTON, D.C."

"State of Missouri, ⎫
County of St. Louis. ⎭ *ss.*

"I, the undersigned Recorder of said county, certify that the foregoing instrument of writing was filed for record in my office on the 14th day of November, 1855; it is truly recorded in Book No. 169, page 288.

"Witness my hand and official seal, date last aforesaid.

[L.S.]   " C. KEEMLE, *Recorder.*"

CHAPTER IV.

IN THE FAMILY OF SENATOR JEFFERSON DAVIS.

THE twelve hundred dollars with which I purchased the freedom of myself and son I consented to accept only as a loan. I went to work in earnest, and in a short time paid every cent that was so kindly advanced by my lady patrons of St Louis. All this time my husband was a source of trouble to me, and a burden. Too close occupation with my needle had its effects upon my health, and feeling exhausted with work, I determined to make a change. I had a conversation with Mr. Keckley; informed

him that since he persisted in dissipation we
must separate; that I was going North, and that
I should never live with him again, at least until
I had good evidence of his reform. He was
rapidly debasing himself, and although I was
willing to work for him, I was not willing to
share his degradation. Poor man; he had his
faults, but over these faults death has drawn a
veil. My husband is now sleeping in his grave,
and in the silent grave I would bury all un-
pleasant memories of him.

I left St. Louis in the spring of 1860,
taking the cars direct for Baltimore, where
I stopped six weeks, attempting to realize a
sum of money by forming classes of young
colored women, and teaching them my system
of cutting and fitting dresses. The scheme was
not successful, for after six weeks of labor and
vexation, I left Baltimore with scarcely money
enough to pay my fare to Washington. Arriving
in the capital, I sought and obtained work at two

dollars and a half per day. However, as I was
notified that I could only remain in the city ten
days without obtaining a license to do so, such
being the law, and as I did not know whom to apply to for assistance, I was sorely troubled. I also
had to have some one vouch to the authorities that
I was a free woman. My means were too scanty,
and my profession too precarious to warrant my
purchasing license. In my perplexity I called on
a lady for whom I was sewing, Miss Ringold, a
member of Gen. Mason's family, from Virginia.
I stated my case, and she kindly volunteered to
render me all the assistance in her power. She
called on Mayor Burritt with me, and Miss
Ringold succeeded in making an arrangement for
me to remain in Washington without paying the
sum required for a license; moreover, I was not
to be molested. I rented apartments in a good
locality, and soon had a good run of custom.
The summer passed, winter came, and I was still
in Washington. Mrs. Davis, wife of Senator Jef-

ferson Davis, came from the South in November
of 1860, with her husband. Learning that Mrs.
Davis wanted a modiste, I presented myself, and
was employed by her on the recommendation of
one of my patrons and her intimate friend, Mrs.
Captain Hetsill. I went to the house to work,
but finding that they were such late risers, and as
I had to fit many dresses on Mrs. Davis, I told
her that I should prefer giving half the day to
her, working the other in my own room for some
of my other lady patrons. Mrs. D. consented to
the proposition, and it was arranged that I should
come to her own house every day after 12 M.
It was the winter before the breaking out of that
fierce and bloody war between the two sections
of the country; and as Mr. Davis occupied a
leading position, his house was the resort of
politicians and statesmen from the South.
Almost every night, as I learned from the
servants and other members of the family, secret
meetings were held at the house; and some of

these meetings were protracted to a very late
hour. The prospects of war were freely discussed in my presence by Mr. and Mrs. Davis and
their friends. The holidays were approaching,
and Mrs. Davis kept me busy in manufacturing
articles of dress for herself and children. She
desired to present Mr. Davis on Christmas with
a handsome dressing-gown. The material was
purchased, and for weeks the work had been
under way. Christmas eve came, and the gown
had been laid aside so often that it was still un-
finished. I saw that Mrs. D. was anxious to
have it completed, so I volunteered to remain
and work on it. Wearily the hours dragged on,
but there was no rest for my busy fingers. I
persevered in my task, notwithstanding my head
was aching. Mrs. Davis was busy in the adjoining room, arranging the Christmas tree for the
children. I looked at the clock, and the hands
pointed to a quarter of twelve. I was arranging
the cords on the gown when the Senator came

in; he looked somewhat careworn, and his step seemed to be a little nervous. He leaned against the door, and expressed his admiration of the Christmas tree, but there was no smile on his face. Turning round, he saw me sitting in the adjoining room, and quickly exclaimed:

"That you, Lizzie! why are you here so late? Still at work; I hope that Mrs. Davis is not too exacting!"

"No, sir," I answered. "Mrs. Davis was very anxious to have this gown finished to-night, and I volunteered to remain and complete it."

"Well, well, the case must be urgent," and he came slowly towards me, took the gown in his hand, and asked the color of the silk, as he said the gas-light was so deceptive to his old eyes.

"It is a drab changeable silk, Mr. Davis," I answered; and might have added that it was rich and handsome, but did not, well knowing that he would make the discovery in the morning.

He smiled curiously, but turned and walked

from the room without another question. He
inferred that the gown was for him, that it was to
be the Christmas present from his wife, and he
did not wish to destroy the pleasure that she
would experience in believing that the gift would
prove a surprise. In this respect, as in many
others, he always appeared to me as a thoughtful,
considerate man in the domestic circle. As the
clock struck twelve I finished the gown, little
dreaming of the future that was before it. It
was worn, I have not the shadow of a doubt, by
Mr. Davis during the stormy years that he was
the President of the Confederate States.

The holidays passed, and before the close of
January the war was discussed in Mr. Davis's
family as an event certain to happen in the
future. Mrs. Davis was warmly attached to
Washington, and I often heard her say that she
disliked the idea of breaking up old associations,
and going South to suffer from trouble and de-
privation. One day, while discussing the ques-

tion in my presence with one of her intimate friends, she exclaimed: "I would rather remain in Washington and be kicked about, than go South and be Mrs. President." Her friend expressed surprise at the remark, and Mrs. Davis insisted that the opinion was an honest one.

While dressing her one day, she said to me: "Lizzie, you are so very handy that I should like to take you South with me."

"When do you go South, Mrs. Davis?" I inquired.

"Oh, I cannot tell just now, but it will be soon. You know there is going to be war, Lizzie?"

"No!"

"But I tell you yes."

"Who will go to war?" I asked.

"The North and South," was her ready reply. "The Southern people will not submit to the humiliating demands of the Abolition party; they will fight first."

"And which do you think will whip?"

"The South, of course. The South is impulsive, is in earnest, and the Southern soldiers will fight to conquer. The North will yield, when it sees the South is in earnest, rather than engage in a long and bloody war."

"But, Mrs. Davis, are you certain that there will be war?"

"Certain!—I know it. You had better go South with me; I will take good care of you. Besides, when the war breaks out, the colored people will suffer in the North. The Northern people will look upon them as the cause of the war, and I fear, in their exasperation, will be inclined to treat you harshly. Then, I may come back to Washington in a few months, and live in the White House. The Southern people talk of choosing Mr. Davis for their President. In fact, it may be considered settled that he will be their President. As soon as we go South and secede from the other States, we will raise an army and march on Washington, and then I shall live in the White House."

I was bewildered with what I heard. I had served Mrs. Davis faithfully, and she had learned to place the greatest confidence in me. At first I was almost tempted to go South with her, for her reasoning seemed plausible. At the time the conversation was closed, with my promise to consider the question.

I thought over the question much, and the more I thought the less inclined I felt to accept the proposition so kindly made by Mrs. Davis. I knew the North to be strong, and believed that the people would fight for the flag that they pretended to venerate so highly. The Republican party had just emerged from a heated campaign, flushed with victory, and I could not think that the hosts composing the party would quietly yield all they had gained in the Presidential canvass. A show of war from the South, I felt, would lead to actual war in the North; and with the two sections bitterly arrayed against each other, I preferred to cast my lot among the people of the North.

I parted with Mrs. Davis kindly, half promising to join her in the South if further deliberation should induce me to change my views. A few weeks before she left Washington I made two chintz wrappers for her. She said that she must give up expensive dressing for a while; and that she, with the Southern people, now that war was imminent, must learn to practise lessons of economy. She left some fine needle-work in my hands, which I finished, and forwarded to her at Montgomery, Alabama, in the month of June, through the assistance of Mrs. Emory, one of her oldest and best friends.

Since bidding them good-by at Washington, early in the year 1860, I have never met any of the Davis family. Years of excitement, years of bloodshed, and hundreds of thousands of graves intervene between the months I spent in the

4

family and now. The years have brought many changes; and in view of these terrible changes even I, who was once a slave, who have been punished with the cruel lash, who have experienced the heart and soul tortures of a slave's life, can say to Mr. Jefferson Davis, "Peace! you have suffered! Go in peace."

In the winter of 1865 I was in Chicago, and one day visited the great charity fair held for the benefit of the families of those soldiers who were killed or wounded during the war. In one part of the building was a wax figure of Jefferson Davis, wearing over his other garments the dress in which it was reported that he was captured. There was always a great crowd around this figure, and I was naturally attracted towards it. I worked my way to the figure, and in examining the dress made the pleasing discovery that it was one of the chintz wrappers that I had made for Mrs. Davis, a short time before she departed from Washington for the South.   When it was announced tuat I recognized the dress as one that I had made for the wife of the late Confederate President there was great cheering and excitement, and I at once became an object of the deepest curiosity.   Great crowds followed me, and in order to escape from the embarrassing situation I left the building.

I believe it now is pretty well established that Mr. Davis had on a water-proof cloak instead of a dress, as first reported, when he was captured. This does not invalidate any portion of my story. The dress on the wax figure at the fair in Chicago unquestionably was one of the chintz wrappers that I made for Mrs. Davis in January, 1860, in Washington; and I infer, since it was not found on the body of the fugitive President of the South, it was taken from the trunks of Mrs. Davis, captured at the same time.   Be this as it may, the coincidence is none the less striking and curious.

CHAPTER V.

MY INTRODUCTION TO MRS. LINCOLN.

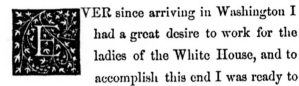 VER since arriving in Washington I
had a great desire to work for the
ladies of the White House, and to
accomplish this end I was ready to
make almost any sacrifice consistent with propriety. Work came in slowly, and I was beginning to feel very much embarrassed, for I did
not know how I was to meet the bills staring me
in the face. It is true, the bills were small, but
then they were formidable to me, who had little
or nothing to pay them with. While in this situation I called at the Ringolds, where I met Mrs.

Captain Lee. Mrs. L. was in a state bordering on excitement, as the great event of the season, the dinner-party given in honor of the Prince of Wales, was soon to come off, and she must have a dress suitable for the occasion. The silk had been purchased, but a dress-maker had not yet been found. Miss Ringold recommended me, and I received the order to make the dress. When I called on Mrs. Lee the next day, her husband was in the room, and handing me a roll of bank bills, amounting to one hundred dollars, he requested me to purchase the trimmings, and to spare no expense in making a selection. With the money in my pocket I went out in the street, entered the store of Harper & Mitchell, and asked to look at their laces. Mr. Harper waited on me himself, and was polite and kind. When I asked permission to carry the laces to Mrs. Lee, in order to learn whether she could approve my selection or not, he gave a ready assent. When I reminded him that I was a stranger, and that the goods were valuable, he remarked that he was not afraid to trust me—that he believed my face was the index to an honest heart. It was pleasant to be spoken to thus, and I shall never forget the kind words of Mr. Harper. I often recall them, for they are associated with the dawn of a brighter period in my dark life. I purchased the trimmings, and Mr. Harper allowed me a commission of twenty-five dollars on the purchase. The dress was done in time, and it gave complete satisfaction. Mrs. Lee attracted great attention at the dinner-party, and her elegant dress proved a good card for me. I received numerous orders, and was relieved from all pecuniary embarrassments. One of my patrons was Mrs. Gen. McClean, a daughter of Gen. Sumner. One day when I was very busy, Mrs. McC. drove up to my apartments, came in where I was engaged with my needle, and in her emphatic way said:

"Lizzie, I am invited to dine at Willard's on

next Sunday, and positively I have not a dress
fit to wear on the occasion. I have just purchased material, and you must commence work
on it right away."

"But Mrs. McClean," I replied, "I have more
work now promised than I can do. It is impossible for me to make a dress for you to wear on
Sunday next."

"Pshaw! Nothing is impossible. I must
have the dress made by Sunday;" and she spoke
with some impatience.

"I am sorry," I began, but she interrupted
me.

"Now don't say no again. I tell you that
you must make the dress. I have often heard
you say that you would like to work for the
ladies of the White House. Well, I have it in
my power to obtain you this privilege. I know
Mrs. Lincoln well, and you shall make a dress
for her provided you finish mine in time to wear
at dinner on Sunday."

The inducement was the best that could have been offered. I would undertake the dress if I should have to sit up all night—every night, to make my pledge good. I sent out and employed assistants, and, after much worry and trouble, the dress was completed to the satisfaction of Mrs. McClean. It appears that Mrs. Lincoln had upset a cup of coffee on the dress she designed wearing on the evening of the reception after the inauguration of Abraham Lincoln as President of the United States, which rendered it necessary that she should have a new one for the occasion. On asking Mrs. McClean who her dress-maker was, that lady promptly informed her,

"Lizzie Keckley."

"Lizzie Keckley? The name is familiar to me. She used to work for some of my lady friends in St. Louis, and they spoke well of her. Can you recommend her to me?"

"With confidence. Shall I send her to you?"

"If you please. I shall feel under many obligations for your kindness."

The next Sunday Mrs. McClean sent me a message to call at her house at four o'clock P.M., that day. As she did not state why I was to call, I determined to wait till Monday morning. Monday morning came, and nine o'clock found me at Mrs. McC.'s house. The streets of the capital were thronged with people, for this was Inauguration day. A new President, a man of the people from the broad prairies of the West, was to accept the solemn oath of office, was to assume the responsibilities attached to the high position of Chief Magistrate of the United States. Never was such deep interest felt in the inauguration proceedings as was felt to-day; for threats of assassination had been made, and every breeze from the South came heavily laden with the rumors of war. Around Willard's hotel swayed an excited crowd, and it was with the utmost difficulty that I worked my way to the

4*

house on the opposite side of the street, occupied by the McCleans. Mrs. McClean was out, but presently an aide on General McClean's staff called, and informed me that I was wanted at Willard's. I crossed the street, and on entering the hotel was met by Mrs. McClean, who greeted me:

"Lizzie, why did you not come yesterday, as I requested? Mrs. Lincoln wanted to see you, but I fear that now you are too late."

"I am sorry, Mrs. McClean. You did not say what you wanted with me yesterday, so I judged that this morning would do as well."

"You should have come yesterday," she insisted. "Go up to Mrs. Lincoln's room"—giving me the number—"she may find use for you yet."

With a nervous step I passed on, and knocked at Mrs. Lincoln's door. A cheery voice bade me come in, and a lady, inclined to stoutness, about forty years of age, stood before me.

"You are Lizzie Keckley, I believe."

I bowed assent.

"The dress-maker that Mrs. McClean recommended?"

"Yes, madam."

"Very well; I have not time to talk to you now, but would like to have you call at the White House, at eight o'clock to-morrow morning, where I shall then be."

I bowed myself out of the room, and returned to my apartments. The day passed slowly, for I could not help but speculate in relation to the appointed interview for the morrow. My long-cherished hope was about to be realized, and I could not rest.

Tuesday morning, at eight o'clock, I crossed the threshold of the White House for the first time. I was shown into a waiting-room, and informed that Mrs. Lincoln was at breakfast. In the waiting-room I found no less than three mantua-makers waiting for an interview with the

wife of the new President. It seems that Mrs.
Lincoln had told several of her lady friends that
she had urgent need for a dress-maker, and that
each of these friends had sent her mantua-maker
to the White House. Hope fell at once. With
so many rivals for the position sought after, I regarded my chances for success as extremely doubt-
ful. I was the last one summoned to Mrs. Lincoln's presence. All the others had a hearing,
and were dismissed. I went up-stairs timidly,
and entering the room with nervous step, discovered the wife of the President standing by a
window, looking out, and engaged in lively conversation with a lady, Mrs. Grimsly, as I afterwards learned. Mrs. L. came forward, and greeted me warmly.

" You have come at last.   Mrs. Keckley, who
have you worked for in the city ?"

" Among others, Mrs. Senator Davis has been
one of my best patrons," was my reply.

"Mrs. Davis ! So you have worked for her,

have you? Of course you gave satisfaction; so far, good. Can you do my work?"

"Yes, Mrs. Lincoln. Will you have much work for me to do?"

"That, Mrs. Keckley, will depend altogether upon your prices. I trust that your terms are reasonable. I cannot afford to be extravagant. We are just from the West, and are poor. If you do not charge too much, I shall be able to give you all my work."

"I do not think there will be any difficulty about charges, Mrs. Lincoln; my terms are reasonable."

"Well, if you will work cheap, you shall have plenty to do. I can't afford to pay big prices, so I frankly tell you so in the beginning."

The terms were satisfactorily arranged, and I measured Mrs. Lincoln, took the dress with me, a bright rose-colored moire-antique, and returned the next day to fit it on her. A number of ladies were in the room, all making preparations for the levee to come off on Friday night. These ladies, I learned, were relatives of Mrs. L.'s,—Mrs. Edwards and Mrs. Kellogg, her own sisters, and Elizabeth Edwards and Julia Baker, her nieces. Mrs. Lincoln this morning was dressed in a cashmere wrapper, quilted down the front; and she wore a simple head-dress. The other ladies wore morning robes.

I was hard at work on the dress, when I was informed that the levee had been postponed from Friday night till Tuesday night. This, of course, gave me more time to complete my task. Mrs. Lincoln sent for me, and suggested some alteration in style, which was made. She also requested that I make a waist of blue watered silk for Mrs. Grimsly, as work on the dress would not require all my time.

Tuesday evening came, and I had taken the last stitches on the dress. I folded it and carried it to the White House, with the waist for Mrs. Grimsly. When I went up-stairs, I found the ladies in a terrible state of excitement. Mrs. Lincoln was protesting that she could not go down, for the reason that she had nothing to wear.

" Mrs. Keckley, you have disappointed me—deceived me. Why do you bring my dress at this late hour ? "

" Because I have just finished it, and I thought I should be in time."

" But you are not in time, Mrs. Keckley; you have bitterly disappointed me. I have no time now to dress, and, what is more, I will not dress, and go down-stairs."

" I am sorry if I have disappointed you, Mrs. Lincoln, for I intended to be in time. Will you let me dress you ? I can have you ready in a few minutes."

" No, I won't be dressed. I will stay in my room. Mr. Lincoln can go down with the other ladies."

" But there is plenty of time for you to dress,

Mary," joined in Mrs. Grimsly and Mrs. Edwards. " Let Mrs. Keckley assist you, and she will soon have you ready."

Thus urged, she consented. I dressed her hair, and arranged the dress on her. It fitted nicely, and she was pleased. Mr. Lincoln came in, threw himself on the sofa, laughed with Willie and little Tad, and then commenced pulling on his gloves, quoting poetry all the while.

" You seem to be in a poetical mood to-night," said his wife.

" Yes, mother, these are poetical times," was his pleasant reply. " I declare, you look charming in that dress. Mrs. Keckley has met with great success." And then he proceeded to compliment the other ladies

Mrs. Lincoln looked elegant in her rose-colored moire-antique. She wore a pearl necklace, pearl ear-rings, pearl bracelets, and red roses in her hair. Mrs. Baker was dressed in lemon-colored silk; Mrs. Kellogg in a drab silk, ashes of rose;

Mrs. Edwards in a brown and black silk; Miss Edwards in crimson, and Mrs. Grimsly in blue watered silk.   Just before starting down-stairs, Mrs. Lincoln's lace handkerchief was the object of search.   It had been displaced by Tad, who was mischievous, and hard to restrain.   The handkerchief found, all became serene.   Mrs. Lincoln took the President's arm, and with smiling face led the train below.   I was surprised at her grace and composure.   I had heard so much, in current and malicious report, of her low life, of her ignorance and vulgarity, that I expected to see her embarrassed on this occasion.   Report, I soon saw, was wrong.   No queen, accustomed to the usages of royalty all her life, could have comported herself with more calmness and dignity than did the wife of the President.   She was confident and self-possessed, and confidence always gives grace.

This levee was a brilliant one, and the only one of the season.   I became the regular modiste

of Mrs. Lincoln.   I made fifteen or sixteen
dresses for her during the spring and early part
of the summer, when she left Washington;
spending the hot weather at Saratoga, Long
Branch, and other places.   In the mean time I
was employed by Mrs. Senator Douglas, one of
the loveliest ladies that I ever met, Mrs. Secretary
Wells, Mrs. Secretary Stanton, and others.   Mrs.
Douglas always dressed in deep mourning, with
excellent taste, and several of the leading ladies
of Washington society were extremely jealous of
her superior attractions.

CHAPTER VI.

WILLIE LINCOLN'S DEATH-BED.

RS. LINCOLN returned to Washington in November, and again duty called me to the White House. The war was now in progress, and every day brought stirring news from the front —the front, where the Gray opposed the Blue, where flashed the bright sabre in the sunshine, where were heard the angry notes of battle, the deep roar of cannon, and the fearful rattle of musketry; where new graves were being made every day, where brother forgot a mother's early blessing and sought the life-blood of brother, and friend raised the deadly knife against friend.

Oh, the front, with its stirring battle-scenes!
Oh, the front, with its ghastly heaps of dead!
The life of the nation was at stake; and when the
land was full of sorrow, there could not be much
gayety at the capital. The days passed quietly
with me. I soon learned that some people had an
intense desire to penetrate the inner circle of the
White House. No President and his family,
heretofore occupying this mansion, ever excited
so much curiosity as the present incumbents.
Mr. Lincoln had grown up in the wilds of the
West, and evil report had said much of him and
his wife. The polite world was shocked, and the
tendency to exaggerate intensified curiosity. As
soon as it was known that I was the modiste of
Mrs. Lincoln, parties crowded around and affected friendship for me, hoping to induce me to betray the secrets of the domestic circle. One day
a woman, I will not call her a lady, drove up to
my rooms, gave me an order to make a dress, and
insisted on partly paying me in advance. She

called on me every day, and was exceedingly
kind. When she came to take her dress away,
she cautiously remarked:

"Mrs. Keckley, you know Mrs. Lincoln?"

"Yes."

"You are her modiste; are you not?"

"Yes."

"You know her very well; do you not?"

"I am with her every day or two."

"Don't you think you would have some influence with her?"

"I cannot say. Mrs. Lincoln, I presume,
would listen to anything I should suggest, but
whether she would be influenced by a suggestion
of mine is another question."

"I am sure that you could influence her, Mrs.
Keckley. Now listen; I have a proposition to
make. I have a great desire to become an in-
mate of the White House. I have heard so
much of Mr. Lincoln's goodness that I should
like to be near him; and if I can enter the

White House no other way, I am willing to go as a menial. My dear Mrs. Keckley, will you not recommend me to Mrs. Lincoln as a friend of yours out of employment, and ask her to take me as a chambermaid? If you will do this you shall be well rewarded. It may be worth several thousand dollars to you in time."

I looked at the woman in amazement. A bribe, and to betray the confidence of my employer! Turning to her with a glance of scorn, I said:

"Madam, you are mistaken in regard to my character. Sooner than betray the trust of a friend, I would throw myself into the Potomac river. I am not so base as that. Pardon me, but there is the door, and I trust that you will never enter my room again."

She sprang to her feet in deep confusion, and passed through the door, murmuring: "Very well; you will live to regret your action to-day."

"Never, never!" I exclaimed, and closed the door after her with a bang. I afterwards learned that this woman was an actress, and that her object was to enter the White House as a servant, learn its secrets, and then publish a scandal to the world. I do not give her name, for such publicity would wound the sensitive feelings of friends, who would have to share her disgrace, without being responsible for her faults. I simply record the incident to show how I often was approached by unprincipled parties. It is unnecessary to say that I indignantly refused every bribe offered.

The first public appearance of Mrs. Lincoln that winter was at the reception on New Year's Day. This reception was shortly followed by a brilliant levee. The day after the levee I went to the White House, and while fitting a dress to Mrs. Lincoln, she said:

"Lizabeth"—she had learned to drop the E— "Lizabeth, I have an idea. These are war times, and we must be as economical as possible. You know the President is expected to give a series of state dinners every winter, and these dinners are very costly; Now I want to avoid this expense; and my idea is, that if I give three large receptions, the state dinners can be scratched from the programme. What do you think, Lizabeth ? "

"I think that you are right, Mrs. Lincoln."

"I am glad to hear you say so. If I can make Mr. Lincoln take the same view of the case, I shall not fail to put the idea into practice."

Before I left her room that day, Mr. Lincoln came in. She at once stated the case to him. He pondered the question a few moments before answering.

"Mother, I am afraid your plan will not work."

"But it *will* work, if you will only determine that it *shall* work."

"It is breaking in on the regular custom," he mildly replied.

"But you forget, father, these are war times, and old customs can be done away with for the once. The idea is economical, you must admit."

"Yes, mother, but we must think of something besides economy."

"I do think of something else. Public receptions are more democratic than stupid state dinners—are more in keeping with the spirit of the institutions of our country, as you would say if called upon to make a stump speech. There are a great many strangers in the city, foreigners and others, whom we can entertain at our receptions, but whom we cannot invite to our dinners."

"I believe you are right, mother. You argue the point well. I think that we shall have to decide on the receptions."

So the day was carried. The question was decided, and arrangements were made for the first reception. It now was January, and cards were issued for February.

5

The children, Tad and Willie, were constantly receiving presents. Willie was so delighted with a little pony, that he insisted on riding it every day. The weather was changeable, and exposure resulted in a severe cold, which deepened into fever. He was very sick, and I was summoned to his bedside. It was sad to see the poor boy suffer. Always of a delicate constitution, he could not resist the strong inroads of disease. The days dragged wearily by, and he grew weaker and more shadow-like. He was his mother's favorite child, and she doted on him. It grieved her heart sorely to see him suffer. When able to be about, he was almost constantly by her side. When I would go in her room, almost always I found blue-eyed Willie there, reading from an open book, or curled up in a chair with pencil and paper in hand. He had decidedly a literary taste, and was a studious boy. A short time before his death he wrote this simple little poem:

"WASHINGTON, D. C., October 30, 1861.

"DEAR SIR :—I enclose you my first attempt at poetry.

"Yours truly,

"WM. W. LINCOLN.

"*To the Editor of the National Republican.*"

LINES
ON THE DEATH OF COLONEL EDWARD BAKER.

THERE was no patriot like Baker,
    So noble and so true;
He fell as a soldier on the field,
    His face to the sky of blue.

His voice is silent in the hall
    Which oft his presence graced;
No more he'll hear the loud acclaim
    Which rang from place to place.

No squeamish notions filled his breast,
    The Union was his theme;
No surrender and no compromise,"
    His day-thought and night's dream.

His Country has *her* part to pay
To'rds those he has left behind;
His widow and his children all,
She must always keep in mind.

Finding that Willie continued to grow worse,
Mrs. Lincoln determined to withdraw her cards
of invitation and postpone the reception. Mr.
Lincoln thought that the cards had better not be
withdrawn. At least he advised that the doctor
be consulted before any steps were taken. Accordingly Dr. Stone was called in. He pro-
nounced Willie better, and said that there was
every reason for an early recovery. He thought,
since the invitations had been issued, it would be
best to go on with the reception. Willie, he
insisted, was in no immediate danger. Mrs.
Lincoln was guided by these counsels, and no
postponement was announced. On the evening
of the reception Willie was suddenly taken
worse His mother sat by his bedside a long
while, holding his feverish hand in her own, and

watching his labored breathing. The doctor claimed there was no cause for alarm. I arranged Mrs. Lincoln's hair, then assisted her to dress. Her dress was white satin, trimmed with black lace. The trail was very long, and as she swept through the room, Mr. Lincoln was standing with his back to the fire, his hands behind him, and his eyes on the carpet. His face wore a thoughtful, solemn look. The rustling of the satin dress attracted his attention. He looked at it a few moments; then, in his quaint, quiet way remarked—

"Whew! our cat has a long tail to-night."

Mrs. Lincoln did not reply. The President added:

"Mother, it is my opinion, if some of that tail was nearer the head, it would be in better style;" and he glanced at her bare arms and neck. She had a beautiful neck and arm, and low dresses were becoming to her. She turned away with a look of offended dignity, and presently took the President's arm, and both went down-stairs to their guests, leaving me alone with the sick boy.

The reception was a large and brilliant one, and the rich notes of the Marine Band in the apartments below came to the sick-room in soft, subdued murmurs, like the wild, faint sobbing of far-off spirits. Some of the young people had suggested dancing, but Mr. Lincoln met the suggestion with an emphatic veto. The brilliance of the scene could not dispel the sadness that rested upon the face of Mrs. Lincoln. During the evening she came up-stairs several times, and stood by the bedside of the suffering boy. She loved him with a mother's heart, and her anxiety was great. The night passed slowly; morning came, and Willie was worse. He lingered a few days, and died. God called the beautiful spirit home, and the house of joy was turned into the house of mourning. I was worn out with watch-ing, and was not in the room when Willie died, but was immediately sent for. I assisted in washing him and dressing him, and then laid him on the bed, when Mr. Lincoln came in. I never saw a man so bowed down with grief. He came to the bed, lifted the cover from the face of his child, gazed at it long and earnestly, murmuring, " My poor boy, he was too good for this earth. God has called him home. I know that he is much better off in heaven, but then we loved him so. It is hard, hard to have him die ! "

Great sobs choked his utterance. He buried his head in his hands, and his tall frame was convulsed with emotion. I stood at the foot of the bed, my eyes full of tears, looking at the man in silent, awe-stricken wonder. His grief unnerved him, and made him a weak, passive child. I did not dream that his rugged nature could be so moved. I shall never forget those solemn moments—genius and greatness weeping over love's idol lost. There is a grandeur as well as a simplicity about the picture that will never fade. With me it is immortal—I really believe that I shall carry it with me across the dark, mysterious river of death.

Mrs. Lincoln's grief was inconsolable. The pale face of her dead boy threw her into convulsions. Around him love's tendrils had been twined, and now that he was dressed for the tomb, it was like tearing the tendrils out of the heart by their roots. Willie, she often said, if spared by Providence, would be the hope and stay of her old age. But Providence had not spared him. The light faded from his eyes, and the death-dew had gathered on his brow.

In one of her paroxysms of grief the President kindly bent over his wife, took her by the arm, and gently led her to the window. With a stately, solemn gesture, he pointed to the lunatic asylum.

"Mother, do you see that large white building on the hill yonder? Try and control your grief, or it will drive you mad, and we may have to send you there."

Mrs. Lincoln was so completely overwhelmed with sorrow that she did not attend the funeral. Willie was laid to rest in the cemetery, and the White House was draped in mourning. Black crape everywhere met the eye, contrasting strangely with the gay and brilliant colors of a few days before. Party dresses were laid aside, and every one who crossed the threshold of the Presidential mansion spoke in subdued tones when they thought of the sweet boy at rest—

" Under the sod and the dew."

Previous to this I had lost my son. Leaving Wilberforce, he went to the battle-field with the three months troops, and was killed in Missouri —found his grave on the battle-field where the gallant General Lyon fell. It was a sad blow to me, and the kind womanly letter that Mrs. Lincoln wrote to me when she heard of my bereavement was full of golden words of comfort.

5*

Nathaniel Parker Willis, the genial poet, now sleeping in his grave, wrote this beautiful sketch of Willie Lincoln, after the sad death of the bright-eyed boy:

"This little fellow had his acquaintances among his father's friends, and I chanced to be one of them. He never failed to seek me out in the crowd, shake hands, and make some pleasant remark; and this, in a boy of ten years of age, was, to say the least, endearing to a stranger. But he had more than mere affectionateness. His self-possession—*aplomb*, as the French call it—was extraordinary. I was one day passing the White House, when he was outside with a play-fellow on the side-walk. Mr. Seward drove in, with Prince Napoleon and two of his *suite* in the carriage; and, in a mock-heroic way—terms of intimacy evidently existing between the boy and the Secretary—the official gentleman took off his hat, and the Napoleon did the same, all making the young Prince President a ceremonious salute. Not a bit staggered with the homage, Willie drew himself up to his full height, took off his little cap with graceful self-possession, and bowed down formally to the ground, like a little ambassador. They drove past, and he went on unconcernedly with his play: the impromptu readiness and good judgment being clearly a part of his nature. His genial and open expression of countenance was none the less ingenuous and fearless for a certain tincture of fun; and it was in this mingling of qualities that he so faithfully resembled his father.

"With all the splendor that was around this little fellow in his new home, he was so bravely and beautifully *himself*—and that only. A wild flower transplanted from the prairie to the hot-house, he retained his prairie habits, unalterably pure and simple, till he died. His leading trait seemed to be a fearless and kindly frankness, willing that everything should be as different as it pleased, but resting unmoved in his own con-

scious single-heartedness. I found I was study
ing him irresistibly, as one of the sweet problems
of childhood that the world is blessed with in
rare places; and the news of his death (I was
absent from Washington, on a visit to my own
children, at the time) came to me like a knell
heard unexpectedly at a merry-making.

"On the day of the funeral I went before the
hour, to take a near farewell look at the dear
boy; for they had embalmed him to send home
to the West—to sleep under the sod of his own
valley—and the coffin-lid was to be closed before the service. The family had just taken
their leave of him, and the servants and nurses
were seeing him for the last time—and with
tears and sobs wholly unrestrained, for he was
loved like an idol by every one of them. He
lay with eyes closed—his brown hair parted as
we had known it—pale in the slumber of death;
but otherwise unchanged, for he was dressed as
if for the evening, and held in one of his hands,

crossed upon his breast, a bunch of exquisite flowers—a message coming from his mother, while we were looking upon him, that those flowers might be preserved for her. She was lying sick in her bed, worn out with grief and overwatching.

" The funeral was very touching. Of the entertainments in the East Room the boy had been —for those who now assembled more especially —a most life-giving variation. With his bright face, and his apt greetings and replies, he was remembered in every part of that crimson-curtained hall, built only for pleasure—of all the crowds, each night, certainly the one least likely to be death's first mark. He was his father's favorite. They were intimates—often seen hand in hand. And there sat the man, with a burden on his brain at which the world marvels—bent now with the load at both heart and brain— staggering under a blow like the taking from him of his child! His men of power sat around him—McClellan, with a moist eye when he bowed to the prayer, as I could see from where I stood; and Chase and Seward, with their austere features at work; and senators, and ambassadors, and soldiers, all struggling with their tears—great hearts sorrowing with the President as a stricken man and a brother. That God may give him strength for all his burdens is, I am sure, at present the prayer of a nation."

This sketch was very much admired by Mrs. Lincoln. I copy it from the scrap-book in which she pasted it, with many tears, with her own hands.

CHAPTER VII.

WASHINGTON IN 1862–3.

N the summer of 1862, freedmen began to flock into Washington from
Maryland and Virginia. They
came with a great hope in their
hearts, and with all their worldly goods on their
backs. Fresh from the bonds of slavery, fresh
from the benighted regions of the plantation, they
came to the Capital looking for liberty, and many
of them not knowing it when they found it.
Many good friends reached forth kind hands, but
the North is not warm and impulsive. For one
kind word spoken, two harsh ones were uttered;

there was something repelling in the atmosphere,
and the bright joyous dreams of freedom to the
slave faded—were sadly altered, in the presence
of that stern, practical mother, reality.   Instead
of flowery paths, days of perpetual sunshine, and
bowers hanging with golden fruit, the road was
rugged and full of thorns, the sunshine was eclipsed by shadows, and the mute appeals for help
too often were answered by cold neglect.   Poor
dusky children of slavery, men and women of my
own race—the transition from slavery to freedom
was too sudden for you!   The bright dreams
were too rudely dispelled; you were not prepared
for the new life that opened before you, and the
great masses of the North learned to look upon
your helplessness with indifference—learned to
speak of you as an idle, dependent race.   Reason
should have prompted kinder thoughts.   Charity
is ever kind.

One fair summer evening I was walking the
streets of Washington, accompanied by a friend,

when a band of music was heard in the distance.
We wondered what it could mean, and curiosity
prompted us to find out its meaning. We
quickened our steps, and discovered that it came
from the house of Mrs. Farnham. The yard was
brilliantly lighted, ladies and gentlemen were
moving about, and the band was playing some
of its sweetest airs. We approached the sentinel
on duty at the gate, and asked what was going
on. He told us that it was a festival given for
the benefit of the sick and wounded soldiers in
the city. This suggested an idea to me. If the
white people can give festivals to raise funds for
the relief of suffering soldiers, why should not the
well-to-do colored people go to work to do
something for the benefit of the suffering blacks?
I could not rest. The thought was ever present
with me, and the next Sunday I made a suggestion in the colored church, that a society of
colored people be formed to labor for the benefit
of the unfortunate freedmen. The idea proved

popular, and in two weeks "the Contraband Relief Association" was organized, with forty working members.

In September of 1862, Mrs. Lincoln left Washington for New York, and requested me to follow her in a few days, and join her at the Metropolitan Hotel. I was glad of the opportunity to do so, for I thought that in New York I would be able to do something in the interests of our society. Armed with credentials, I took the train for New York, and went to the Metropolitan, where Mrs. Lincoln had secured accommodations for me. The next morning I told Mrs. Lincoln of my project; and she immediately headed my list with a subscription of $200. I circulated among the colored people, and got them thoroughly interested in the subject, when I was called to Boston by Mrs. Lincoln, who wished to visit her son Robert, attending college in that city. I met Mr. Wendell Phillips, and other Boston philanthropists, who gave me all the assistance in their power. We held a mass meeting at the Colored Baptist Church, Rev. Mr. Grimes, in Boston, raised a sum of money, and organized there a branch society. The society was organized by Mrs. Grimes, wife of the pastor, assisted by Mrs. Martin, wife of Rev. Stella Martin. This branch of the main society, during the war, was able to send us over eighty large boxes of goods, contributed exclusively by the colored people of Boston. Returning to New York, we held a successful meeting at the Shiloh Church, Rev. Henry Highland Garnet, pastor. The Metropolitan Hotel, at that time as now, employed colored help. I suggested the object of my mission to Robert Thompson, Steward of the Hotel, who immediately raised quite a sum of money among the dining-room waiters. Mr. Frederick Douglass contributed $200, besides lecturing for us. Other prominent colored men sent in liberal contributions. From England*

* The Sheffield Anti-Slavery Society of England con-

a large quantity of stores was received. Mrs. Lincoln made frequent contributions, as also did the President. In 1863 I was re-elected President of the Association, which office I continue to hold.

For two years after Willie's death the White House was the scene of no fashionable display. The memory of the dead boy was duly respected. In some things Mrs. Lincoln was an altered woman. Sometimes, when in her room, with no one present but myself, the mere mention of Willie's name would excite her emotion, and any trifling memento that recalled him would move her to tears. She could not bear to look upon his picture; and after his death she never

tributed through Mr. Frederick Douglass, to the Freedmen's Relief Association, $24.00 ; Aberdeen Ladies' Society, $40.00 ; Anti-Slavery Society of Edinburgh, Scotland, $48.00 ; Friends at Bristol, England, $176.00 ; Birmingham Negro's Friend Society, $50.00. Also received through Mr. Charles R. Douglass, from the Birmingham Society, $33.00.

crossed the threshold of the Guest's Room in which he died, or the Green Room in which he was embalmed. There was something supernatural in her dread of these things, and something that she could not explain. Tad's nature was the opposite of Willie's, and he was always regarded as his father's favorite child. His black eyes fairly sparkled with mischief.

The war progressed, fair fields had been stained with blood, thousands of brave men had fallen, and thousands of eyes were weeping for the fallen at home. There were desolate hearthstones in the South as well as in the North, and as the people of my race watched the sanguinary struggle, the ebb and flow of the tide of battle, they lifted their faces Zionward, as if they hoped to catch a glimpse of the Promised Land beyond the sulphureous clouds of smoke which shifted now and then but to reveal ghastly rows of new-made graves. Sometimes the very life of the nation seemed to tremble with the fierce shock of arms. In 1863 the Confederates were flushed with victory, and sometimes it looked as if the proud flag of the Union, the glorious old Stars and Stripes, must yield half its nationality to the tri-barred flag that floated grandly over long columns of gray. These were sad, anxious days to Mr. Lincoln, and those who saw the man in privacy only could tell how much he suffered. One day he came into the room where I was fitting a dress on Mrs. Lincoln. His step was slow and heavy, and his face sad. Like a tired child he threw himself upon a sofa, and shaded his eyes with his hands. He was a complete picture of dejection. Mrs. Lincoln, observing his troubled look, asked :

"Where have you been, father ?"

"To the War Department," was the brief, almost sullen answer.

"Any news ?"

"Yes, plenty of news, but no good news. It is dark, dark everywhere."

He reached forth one of his long arms, and took a small Bible from a stand near the head of the sofa, opened the pages of the holy book, and soon was absorbed in reading them. A quarter of an hour passed, and on glancing at the sofa the face of the President seemed more cheerful. The dejected look was gone, and the countenance was lighted up with new resolution and hope. The change was so marked that I could not but wonder at it, and wonder led to the desire to know what book of the Bible afforded so much comfort to the reader. Making the search for a missing article an excuse, I walked gently around the sofa, and looking into the open book, I discovered that Mr. Lincoln was reading that divine comforter, Job. He read with Christian eagerness, and the courage and hope that he derived from the inspired pages made him a new man. I almost imagined that I could hear the Lord speaking to him from out the whirlwind of battle: " Gird up thy loins now like a man: I will demand of thee, and declare thou unto me." What a sublime picture was this! A ruler of a mighty nation going to the pages of the Bible with simple Christian earnestness for comfort and courage, and finding both in the darkest hours of a nation's calamity. Ponder it, O ye scoffers at God's Holy Word, and then hang your heads for very shame!

Frequent letters were received warning Mr. Lincoln of assassination, but he never gave a second thought to the mysterious warnings. The letters, however, sorely troubled his wife. She seemed to read impending danger in every rustling leaf, in every whisper of the wind.

"Where are you going now, father?" she would say to him, as she observed him putting on his overshoes and shawl.

"I am going over to the War Department, mother, to try and learn some news."

"But, father, you should not go out alone. You know you are surrounded with danger."

"All imagination. What does any one want to harm me for? Don't worry about me, mother, as if I were a little child, for no one is going to molest me;" and with a confident, unsuspecting air he would close the door behind him, descend the stairs, and pass out to his lonely walk.

For weeks, when trouble was anticipated, friends of the President would sleep in the White House to guard him from danger.

Robert would come home every few months, bringing new joy to the family circle. He was very anxious to quit school and enter the army, but the move was sternly opposed by his mother.

"We have lost one son, and his loss is as much as I can bear, without being called upon to make another sacrifice," she would say, when the subject was under discussion.

"But many a poor mother has given up all her sons," mildly suggested Mr. Lincoln, "and our son is not more dear to us than the sons of other people are to their mothers."

6

"That may be; but I cannot bear to have Robert exposed to danger. His services are not required in the field, and the sacrifice would be a needless one."

"The services of every man who loves his country are required in this war. You should take a liberal instead of a selfish view of the question, mother."

Argument at last prevailed, and permission was granted Robert to enter the army. With the rank of Captain and A. D. C. he went to the field, and remained in the army till the close of the war.

I well recollect a little incident that gave me a clearer insight into Robert's character. He was at home at the time the Tom Thumb combination was at Washington. The marriage of little Hop-o'-my-thumb—Charles Stratton—to Miss Warren created no little excitement in the world, and the people of Washington participated in the general curiosity. Some of Mrs. Lincoln's friends made her believe that it was the duty of Mrs. Lincoln to show some attention to the remarkable dwarfs. Tom Thumb had been caressed by royalty in the Old World, and why should not the wife of the President of his native country smile upon him also? Verily, duty is one of the greatest bugbears in life. A hasty reception was arranged, and cards of invitation issued. I had dressed Mrs. Lincoln, and she was ready to go below and receive her guests, when Robert entered his mother's room.

"You are at leisure this afternoon, are you not, Robert?"

"Yes, mother."

"Of course, then, you will dress and come down-stairs."

"No, mother, I do not propose to assist in entertaining Tom Thumb. My notions of duty, perhaps, are somewhat different from yours."

Robert had a lofty soul, and he could not stoop

to all of the follies and absurdities of the ephemeral current of fashionable life.

Mrs. Lincoln's love for her husband sometimes prompted her to act very strangely. She was extremely jealous of him, and if a lady desired to court her displeasure, she could select no surer way to do it than to pay marked attention to the President. These little jealous freaks often were a source of perplexity to Mr. Lincoln. If it was a reception for which they were dressing, he would come into her room to conduct her downstairs, and while pulling on his gloves ask, with a merry twinkle in his eyes:

"Well, mother, who must I talk with to-night—shall it be Mrs. D. ?"

"That deceitful woman! No, you shall not listen to her flattery."

"Well, then, what do you say to Miss C.? She is too young and handsome to practise deceit."

"Young and handsome, you call her! You should not judge beauty for me. No, she is in league with Mrs. D., and you shall not talk with her."

"Well, mother, I must talk with some one. Is there any one that you do not object to?" trying to button his glove, with a mock expression of gravity.

"I don't know as it is necessary that you should talk to anybody in particular. You know well enough, Mr. Lincoln, that I do not approve of your flirtations with silly women, just as if you were a beardless boy, fresh from school."

"But, mother, I insist that I must talk with somebody. I can't stand around like a simpleton, and say nothing. If you will not tell me who I may talk with, please tell me who I may *not* talk with."

"There is Mrs. D. and Miss C. in particular. I detest them both. Mrs. B. also will come around you, but you need not listen to her flattery. These are the ones in particular."

"Very well, mother; now that we have settled the question to your satisfaction, we will go down-stairs;" and always with stately dignity, he proffered his arm and led the way.

CHAPTER VIII.

FTEN Mr. and Mrs. Lincoln discussed the relations of Cabinet
officers, and gentlemen prominent
in politics, in my presence. I soon
learned that the wife of the President had no
love for Mr. Salmon P. Chase, at that time Secretary of the Treasury. She was well versed in
human character, was somewhat suspicious of
those by whom she was surrounded, and often
her judgment was correct. Her intuition about
the sincerity of individuals was more accurate
than that of her husband. She looked beyond,

and read the reflection of action in the future. Her hostility to Mr. Chase was very bitter. She claimed that he was a selfish politician instead of a true patriot, and warned Mr. Lincoln not to trust him too far. The daughter of the Secretary was quite a belle in Washington, and Mrs. Lincoln, who was jealous of the popularity of others, had no desire to build up her social position through political favor to her father. Miss Chase, now Mrs. Senator Sprague, was a lovely woman, and was worthy of all the admiration she received. Mr. Lincoln was more confiding than his wife. He never suspected the fidelity of those who claimed to be his friends. Honest to the very core himself, and frank as a child, he never dreamed of questioning the sincerity of others.

"Father, I do wish that you would inquire a little into the motives of Chase," said his wife one day.

The President was lying carelessly upon a

sofa, holding a newspaper in his hands. "Mother, you are too suspicious. I give you credit for sagacity, but you are disposed to magnify trifles. Chase is a patriot, and one of my best friends."

"Yes, one of your best friends because it is his interest to be so. He is anything for Chase. If he thought he could make anything by it, he would betray you to-morrow."

"I fear that you are prejudiced against the man, mother. I know that you do him injustice."

"Mr. Lincoln, you are either blind or will not see. I am not the only one that has warned you against him."

"True, I receive letters daily from all parts of the country, telling me not to trust Chase; but then these letters are written by the political enemies of the Secretary, and it would be unjust and foolish to pay any attention to them."

"Very well, you will find out some day, if you live long enough, that I have read the man correctly. I only hope that your eyes may not be

6*

opened to the truth when it is too late." The President, as far as I could judge from his conversation with his wife, continued to confide in Mr. Chase to the time of his tragic death.

Mrs. Lincoln was especially severe on Mr. Wm. H. Seward, Secretary of State. She but rarely lost an opportunity to say an unkind word of him.

One morning I went to the White House earlier than usual. Mr. Lincoln was sitting in a chair, reading a paper, stroking with one hand the head of little Tad. I was basting a dress for Mrs. Lincoln. A servant entered, and handed the President a letter just brought by a messenger. He broke the seal, and when he had read the contents his wife asked:

" Who is the letter from, father ? "

" Seward ; I must go over and see him to-day."

" Seward ! I wish you had nothing to do with that man. He cannot be trusted."

" You say the same of Chase. If I listened to you, I should soon be without a Cabinet."

" Better be without it than to confide in some of the men that you do. Seward is worse than Chase. He has no principle.

" Mother, you are mistaken; your prejudices are so violent that you do not stop to reason. Seward is an able man, and the country as well as myself can trust him."

" Father, you are too honest for this world! You should have been born a saint. You will generally find it a safe rule to distrust a disappointed, ambitious politician. It makes me mad to see you sit still and let that hypocrite, Seward, twine you around his finger as if you were a skein of thread."

" It is useless to argue the question, mother. You cannot change my opinion."

Mrs. Lincoln prided herself upon her ability to read character. She was shrewd and far-seeing, and had no patience with the frank, confiding nature of the President.

When Andrew Johnson was urged for military Governor of Tennessee, Mrs. Lincoln bitterly opposed the appointment.

"He is a demagogue," she said, almost fiercely, "and if you place him in power, Mr. Lincoln, mark my words, you will rue it some day."

General McClellan, when made Commander-in-Chief, was the idol of the soldiers, and never was a general more universally popular. "He is a humbug," remarked Mrs. Lincoln one day in my presence.

"What makes you think so, mother?" good-naturedly inquired the President.

"Because he talks so much and does so little. If I had the power I would very soon take off his head, and put some energetic man in his place."

"But I regard McClellan as a patriot and an able soldier. He has been much embarrassed.

The troops are raw, and the subordinate officers inclined to be rebellious. There are too many politicians in the army with shoulder-straps. McClellan is young and popular, and they are jealous of him. They will kill him off if they can."

"McClellan can make plenty of excuse for himself, therefore he needs no advocate in you. If he would only do something, and not promise so much, I might learn to have a little faith in him. I tell you he is a humbug, and you will have to find some man to take his place, that is, if you wish to conquer the South."

Mrs. Lincoln could not tolerate General Grant. "He is a butcher," she would often say, "and is not fit to be at the head of an army."

"But he has been very successful in the field," argued the President.

"Yes, he generally manages to claim a victory, but such a victory! He loses two men to the enemy's one. He has no management, no regard for life. If the war should continue four years longer, and he should remain in power, he would depopulate the North. I could fight an army as well myself. According to his tactics, there is nothing under the heavens to do but to march a new line of men up in front of the rebel breastworks to be shot down as fast as they take their position, and keep marching until the enemy grows tired of the slaughter. Grant, I repeat, is an obstinate fool and a butcher."

"Well, mother, supposing that we give you command of the army. No doubt you would do much better than any general that has been tried." There was a twinkle in the eyes, and a ring of irony in the voice.

I have often heard Mrs. Lincoln say that if Grant should ever be elected President of the United States she would desire to leave the country, and remain absent during his term of office.

It was well known that Mrs. Lincoln's

brothers were in the Confederate army, and for this reason it was often charged that her sympathies were with the South. Those who made the hasty charge were never more widely mistaken.

One morning, on my way to the White House, I heard that Captain Alexander Todd, one of her brothers, had been killed. I did not like to inform Mrs. Lincoln of his death, judging that it would be painful news to her. I had been in her room but a few minutes when she said, with apparent unconcern, "Lizzie, I have just heard that one of my brothers has been killed in the war."

"I also heard the same, Mrs. Lincoln, but hesitated to speak of it, for fear the subject would be a painful one to you."

"You need not hesitate. Of course, it is but natural that I should feel for one so nearly related to me, but not to the extent that you suppose. He made his choice long ago. He decided against my husband, and through him against me. He has been fighting against us; and since he chose to be our deadly enemy, I see no special reason why I should bitterly mourn his death."

I felt relieved, and in subsequent conversations learned that Mrs. Lincoln had no sympathy for the South. "Why should I sympathize with the rebels," she would say; "are they not against me? They would hang my husband to-morrow if it was in their power, and perhaps gibbet me with him. How then can I sympathize with a people at war with me and mine?" She always objected to being thought Southern in feeling.

Mr. Lincoln was generous by nature, and though his whole heart was in the war, he could not but respect the valor of those opposed to him. His soul was too great for the narrow, selfish views of partisanship. Brave by nature himself, he honored bravery in others, even his foes. Time and again I have heard him speak in the highest terms of the soldierly qualities of

such brave Confederate generals as Lee, Stonewall Jackson, and Joseph E. Johnson. Jackson
was his ideal soldier. "He is a brave, honest
Presbyterian soldier," were his words; "what a
pity that we should have to fight such a gallant
fellow! If we only had such a man to lead the
armies of the North, the country would not be
appalled with so many disasters."

As this is a rambling chapter, I will here record
an incident showing his feeling toward Robert E.
Lee. The very morning of the day on which he
was assassinated, his son, Capt. Robert Lincoln,
came into the room with a portrait of General
Lee in his hand. The President took the picture, laid it on a table before him, scanned the
face thoughtfully, and said: "It is a good face;
it is the face of a noble, noble, brave man. I am
glad that the war is over at last." Looking up
at Robert, he continued: "Well, my son, you
have returned safely from the front. The war is
now closed, and we soon will live in peace with

the brave men that have been fighting against us. I trust that the era of good feeling has returned with the war, and that henceforth we shall live in peace. Now listen to me, Robert: you must lay aside your uniform, and return to college. I wish you to read law for three years, and at the end of that time I hope that we will be able to tell whether you will make a lawyer or not." His face was more cheerful than I had seen it for a long while, and he seemed to be in a generous, forgiving mood.

CHAPTER IX.

Behind the Scenes.

OME of the freedmen and freed-women had exaggerated ideas of liberty. To them it was a beauti-ful vision, a land of sunshine, rest, and glorious promise. They flocked to Washington, and since their extravagant hopes were not realized, it was but natural that many of them should bitterly feel their disappointment. The colored people are wedded to associations, and when you destroy these you destroy half of the happiness of their lives. They make a home, and are so fond of it that they prefer it, squalid

though it be, to the comparative ease and luxury
of a shifting, roaming life. Well, the emancipated
slaves, in coming North, left old associations
behind them, and the love for the past was so
strong that they could not find much beauty
in the new life so suddenly opened to them.
Thousands of the disappointed, huddled together
in camps, fretted and pined like children for the
"good old times." In visiting them in the interests of the Relief Society of which I was
president, they would crowd around me with
pitiful stories of distress. Often I heard them
declare that they would rather go back to slavery
in the South, and be with their old masters, than
to enjoy the freedom of the North. I believe
they were sincere in these declarations, because
dependence had become a part of their second
nature, and independence brought with it the
cares and vexations of poverty.

I was very much amused one day at the grave
complaints of a good old, simple-minded wo-

man, fresh from a life of servitude. She had never ventured beyond a plantation until coming North. The change was too radical for her, and she could not exactly understand it. She thought, as many others thought, that Mr. and Mrs. Lincoln were the government, and that the President and his wife had nothing to do but to supply the extravagant wants of every one that applied to them. The wants of this old woman, however, were not very extravagant.

"Why, Missus Keckley," said she to me one day, "I is been here eight months, and Missus Lingom an't even give me one shife. Bliss God, childen, if I had ar know dat de Government, and Mister and Missus Government, was going to do dat ar way, I neber would 'ave comed here in God's wurld. My old missus us't gib me two shifes eber year."

I could not restrain a laugh at the grave manner in which this good old woman entered her protest. Her idea of freedom was two or more old shifts every year. Northern readers may not fully recognize the pith of the joke. On the Southern plantation, the mistress, according to established custom, every year made a present of certain under-garments to her slaves, which articles were always anxiously looked forward to, and thankfully received. The old woman had been in the habit of receiving annually two shifts from her mistress, and she thought the wife of the President of the United States very mean for overlooking this established custom of the plantation.

While some of the emancipated blacks pined for the old associations of slavery, and refused to help themselves, others went to work with commendable energy, and planned with remarkable forethought. They built themselves cabins, and each family cultivated for itself a small patch of ground. The colored people are fond of domestic life, and with them domestication means happy children, a fat pig, a dozen or more chickens, and a garden. Whoever visits the Freedmen's Village now in the vicinity of Washington will discover all of these evidences of prosperity and happiness. The schools are objects of much interest. Good teachers, white and colored, are employed, and whole brigades of bright-eyed dusky children are there taught the common branches of education. These children are studious, and the teachers inform me that their advancement is rapid. I number among my personal friends twelve colored girls employed as teachers in the schools at Washington. The Colored Mission Sabbath School, established through the influence of Gen. Brown at the Fifteenth Street Presbyterian Church, is always an object of great interest to the residents of the Capital, as well as to the hundreds of strangers visiting the city.

In 1864 the receptions again commenced at the White House. For the first two years of Mr. Lincoln's administration, the President selected a lady to join in the promenade with him, which left Mrs. Lincoln free to choose an escort from among the distinguished gentlemen that always surrounded her on such occasions. This custom at last was discontinued by Mrs. Lincoln.

" Lizabeth ! "—I was sewing in her room, and she was seated in a comfortable arm-chair—" Lizabeth, I have been thinking over a little matter. As you are well aware, the President, at every reception, selects a lady to lead the promenade with him. Now it occurs to me that this custom is an absurd one. On such occasions our guests recognize the position of the President as first of all; consequently, he takes the lead in everything; well, now, if they recognize his position they should also recognize mine. I am his wife, and should lead with him. And yet he offers his arm to any other lady in the room, making her first with him and placing me second. The custom is an absurd one, and I mean to abolish it. The dignity that I owe to my position, as Mrs. President, demands that I should not hesitate any longer to act."

Mrs. Lincoln kept her word. Ever after this, she either led the promenade with the President, or the President walked alone or with a gentleman. The change was much remarked, but the reason why it was made, I believe, was never generally known.

In 1864 much doubt existed in regard to the re-election of Mr. Lincoln, and the White House was besieged by all grades of politicians. Mrs. Lincoln was often blamed for having a certain class of men around her.

"I have an object in view, Lizabeth," she said to me in reference to this matter. "In a political canvass it is policy to cultivate every element of strength. These men have influence, and we require influence to re-elect Mr. Lincoln. I will be clever to them until after the election, and then, if we remain at the White House, I will drop every one of them, and let them know very

7

plainly that I only made tools of them. They are an unprincipled set, and I don't mind a little double-dealing with them."

"Does Mr. Lincoln know what your purpose is?" I asked.

"God! no; he would never sanction such a proceeding, so I keep him in the dark, and will tell him of it when all is over. He is too honest to take the proper care of his own interests, so I feel it to be my duty to electioneer for him."

Mr. Lincoln, as every one knows, was far from handsome. He was not admired for his graceful figure and finely moulded face, but for the nobility of his soul and the greatness of his heart. His wife was different. He was wholly unselfish in every respect, and I believe that he loved the mother of his children very tenderly. He asked nothing but affection from her, but did not always receive it. When in one of her wayward impulsive moods, she was apt to say and do things that wounded him deeply. If he had not loved her, she would have been powerless to cloud his thoughtful face, or gild it with a ray of sunshine as she pleased. We are indifferent to those we do not love, and certainly the President was not indifferent to his wife. She often wounded him in unguarded moments, but calm reflection never failed to bring regret.

Mrs. Lincoln was extremely anxious that her husband should be re-elected President of the United States. In endeavoring to make a display becoming her exalted position, she had to incur many expenses. Mr. Lincoln's salary was inadequate to meet them, and she was forced to run in debt, hoping that good fortune would favor her, and enable her to extricate herself from an embarrassing situation. She bought the most expensive goods on credit, and in the summer of 1864 enormous unpaid bills stared her in the face.

"What do you think about the election, Lizabeth?" she said to me one morning.

"I think that Mr. Lincoln will remain in the White House four years longer," I replied, looking up from my work.

"What makes you think so? Somehow I have learned to fear that he will be defeated."

"Because he has been tried, and has proved faithful to the best interests of the country. The people of the North recognize in him an honest man, and they are willing to confide in him, at least until the war has been brought to a close. The Southern people made his election a pretext for rebellion, and now to replace him by some one else, after years of sanguinary war, would look too much like a surrender of the North. So, Mr. Lincoln is certain to be re-elected. He represents a principle, and to maintain this principle the loyal people of the loyal States will vote for him, even if he had no merits to commend him."

"Your view is a plausible one, Lizabeth, and your confidence gives me new hope. If he should be defeated, I do not know what would become of us all. To me, to him, there is more at stake in this election than he dreams of."

"What can you mean, Mrs. Lincoln? I do not comprehend."

"Simply this. I have contracted large debts, of which he knows nothing, and which he will be unable to pay if he is defeated."

"What are your debts, Mrs. Lincoln?"

"They consist chiefly of store bills. I owe altogether about twenty-seven thousand dollars; the principal portion at Stewart's, in New York. You understand, Lizabeth, that Mr. Lincoln has but little idea of the expense of a woman's wardrobe. He glances at my rich dresses, and is happy in the belief that the few hundred dollars that I obtain from him supply all my wants. I must dress in costly materials. The people scrutinize every article that I wear with critical curiosity. The very fact of having grown up in the West, subjects me to more searching observation.

To keep up appearances, I must have money—
more than Mr. Lincoln can spare for me. He is
too honest to make a penny outside of his salary;
consequently I had, and still have, no alternative
but to run in debt."

"And Mr. Lincoln does not even suspect how
much you owe?"

"God, no!"—this was a favorite expression of
hers—"and I would not have him suspect. If
he knew that his wife was involved to the extent
that she is, the knowledge would drive him mad.
He is so sincere and straightforward himself,
that he is shocked by the duplicity of others.
He does not know a thing about any debts, and
I value his happiness, not to speak of my own,
too much to allow him to know anything. This
is what troubles me so much. If he is re-elected,
I can keep him in ignorance of my affairs; but
if he is defeated, then the bills will be sent in,
and he will know all;" and something like a
hysterical sob escaped her.

Mrs. Lincoln sometimes feared that the politicians would get hold of the particulars of her debts, and use them in the Presidential campaign against her husband; and when this thought occurred to her, she was almost crazy with anxiety and fear.

When in one of these excited moods, she would fiercely exclaim—

"The Republican politicians must pay my debts. Hundreds of them are getting immensely rich off the patronage of my husband, and it is but fair that they should help me out of my embarrassment. I will make a demand of them, and when I tell them the facts they cannot refuse to advance whatever money I require."

CHAPTER X.

The Second Inauguration.

RS. LINCOLN came to my apartments one day towards the close of the summer of 1864, to consult me in relation to a dress. And here let me remark, I never approved of ladies, attached to the Presidential household, coming to my rooms. I always thought that it would be more consistent with their dignity to send for me, and let me come to them, instead of their coming to me. I may have peculiar notions about some things, and this may be regarded as one of them. No matter, I have recorded my opinion. I can-

not forget the associations of my early life.
Well, Mrs. Lincoln came to my rooms, and, as
usual, she had much to say about the Presidential
election.

After some conversation, she asked: " Lizzie,
where do you think I will be this time next
summer ? "

" Why, in the White House, of course."

" I cannot believe so. I have no hope of the
re-election of Mr. Lincoln. The canvass is a
heated one, the people begin to murmur at the
war, and every vile charge is brought against my
husband."

" No matter," I replied, " Mr. Lincoln will
be re-elected. I am so confident of it, that I am
tempted to ask a favor of you."

" A favor ! Well, if we remain in the White
House I shall be able to do you many favors.
What is the special favor ? "

" Simply this, Mrs. Lincoln—I should like for
you to make me a present of the right-hand glove

7*

that the President wears at the first public reception after his second inaugural."

"You shall have it in welcome. It will be so filthy when he pulls it off, I shall be tempted to take the tongs and put it in the fire. I cannot imagine, Lizabeth, what you want with such a glove."

"I shall cherish it as a precious memento of the second inauguration of the man who has done so much for my race. He has been a Jehovah to my people—has lifted them out of bondage, and directed their footsteps from darkness into light. I shall keep the glove, and hand it down to posterity."

"You have some strange ideas, Lizabeth. Never mind, you shall have the glove; that is, if Mr. Lincoln continues President after the 4th of March next."

I held Mrs. Lincoln to her promise. That glove is now in my possession, bearing the marks of the thousands of hands that grasped the honest hand of Mr. Lincoln on that eventful night. Alas! it has become a prouder, sadder memento than I ever dreamed—prior to making the request—it would be.

In due time the election came off, and all of my predictions were verified. The loyal States decided that Mr. Lincoln should continue at the nation's helm. Autumn faded, winter dragged slowly by, and still the country resounded with the clash of arms. The South was suffering, yet suffering was borne with heroic determination, and the army continued to present a bold, defiant front. With the first early breath of spring, thousands of people gathered in Washington to witness the second inauguration of Abraham Lincoln as President of the United States. It was a stirring day in the National Capital, and one that will never fade from the memory of those who witnessed the imposing ceremonies. The morning was dark and gloomy; clouds hung like a pall in the sky, as if portending some great disaster. But when the President stepped forward to receive the oath of office, the clouds parted, and a ray of sunshine streamed from the heavens to fall upon and gild his face. It is also said that a brilliant star was seen at noon-day. It was the noon-day of life with Mr. Lincoln, and the star, as viewed in the light of subsequent events, was emblematic of a summons from on high. This was Saturday, and on Monday evening I went to the White House to dress Mrs. Lincoln for the first grand levee. While arranging Mrs. L.'s hair, the President came in. It was the first time I had seen him since the inauguration, and I went up to him, proffering my hand with words of congratulation.

He grasped my outstretched hand warmly, and held it while he spoke: "Thank you. Well, Madam Elizabeth"—he always called me Madam Elizabeth—"I don't know whether I should feel thankful or not. The position brings with it many trials. We do not know what we are destined to pass through. But God will be with us all. I put my trust in God." He dropped my hand, and with solemn face walked across the room and took his seat on the sofa. Prior to this I had congratulated Mrs. Lincoln, and she had answered with a sigh, "Thank you, Elizabeth; but now that we have won the position, I almost wish it were otherwise. Poor Mr. Lincoln is looking so broken-hearted, so completely worn out, I fear he will not get through the next four years." Was it a presentiment that made her take a sad view of the future? News from the front was never more cheering. On every side the Confederates were losing ground, and the lines of blue were advancing in triumph. As I would look out my window almost every day, I could see the artillery going past on its way to the open space of ground, to fire a salute in honor of some new victory. From every point came glorious news of the success of the soldiers that fought for the Union. And yet, in their private chamber, away from the curious eyes of the world, the President and his wife wore sad, anxious faces.

I finished dressing Mrs. Lincoln, and she took the President's arm and went below. It was one of the largest receptions ever held in Washington. Thousands crowded the halls and rooms of the White House, eager to shake Mr. Lincoln by his hand, and receive a gracious smile from his wife. The jam was terrible, and the enthusiasm great. The President's hand was well shaken, and the next day, on visiting Mrs. Lincoln, I received the soiled glove that Mr. Lincoln had worn on his right hand that night.

Many colored people were in Washington, and large numbers had desired to attend the levee, but orders were issued not to admit them. A gentleman, a member of Congress, on his way to the White House, recognized Mr. Frederick Douglass, the eloquent colored orator, on the outskirts of the crowd.

"How do you do, Mr. Douglass? A fearful jam to-night. You are going in, of course?"

"No—that is, no to your last question."

"Not going in to shake the President by the hand! Why, pray?"

"The best reason in the world. Strict orders have been issued not to admit people of color."

"It is a shame, Mr. Douglass, that you should thus be placed under ban. Never mind; wait here, and I will see what can be done."

The gentleman entered the White House, and working his way to the President, asked permission to introduce Mr. Douglass to him.

"Certainly," said Mr. Lincoln. "Bring Mr. Douglass in, by all means. I shall be glad to meet him."

The gentleman returned, and soon Mr. Douglass stood face to face with the President. Mr. Lincoln pressed his hand warmly, saying: "Mr. Douglass, I am glad to meet you. I have long admired your course, and I value your opinions highly."

Mr. Douglass was very proud of the manner in which Mr. Lincoln received him. On leaving the White House he came to a friend's house where a reception was being held, and he related the incident with great pleasure to myself and others.

On the Monday following the reception at the White House, everybody was busy preparing for the grand inaugural ball to come off that night. I was in Mrs. Lincoln's room the greater portion of the day. While dressing her that night, the President came in, and I remarked to him how much Mr. Douglass had been pleased on the night he was presented to Mr. Lincoln. Mrs. L. at once turned to her husband with the inquiry, "Father, why was not Mr. Douglass introduced to me?"

"I do not know.   I thought he was presented."

"But he was not."

"It must have been an oversight then, mother; I am sorry you did not meet him."

I finished dressing her for the ball, and accompanied her to the door. She was dressed magnificently, and entered the ball-room leaning on the arm of Senator Sumner, a gentleman that she very much admired. Mr. Lincoln walked into the ball-room accompanied by two gentlemen. This ball closed the season. It was the last time that the President and his wife ever appeared in public.

Some days after, Mrs. Lincoln, with a party of friends, went to City Point on a visit.

Mrs. Lincoln had returned to Washington prior to the 2d of April. On Monday, April 3d, Mrs. Secretary Harlan came into my room with material for a dress. While conversing with her, I saw artillery pass the window; and as it was on its way to fire a salute, I inferred that good news had been received at the War Department. My reception-room was on one side of the street, and

my work-room on the other side. Inquiring the
cause of the demonstration, we were told that
Richmond had fallen. Mrs. Harlan took one of
my hands in each of her own, and we rejoiced
together. I ran across to my work-room, and
on entering it, discovered that the girls in my
employ also had heard the good news. They
were particularly elated, as it was reported that
the rebel capital had surrendered to colored
troops. I had promised my employées a holiday when Richmond should fall; and now that
Richmond had fallen, they reminded me of my
promise.

I recrossed to my reception-room, and Mrs.
Harlan told me that the good news was enough
for her—she could afford to wait for her dress,
and to give the girls a holiday and a treat, by all
means. She returned to her house, and I joined
my girls in the joy of the long-promised holiday.
We wandered about the streets of the city with
happy faces, and hearts overflowing with joy.

The clerks in the various departments also enjoyed a holiday, and they improved it by getting gloriously fuddled. Towards evening I saw S., and many other usually clear-headed men, in the street, in a confused, uncertain state of mind.

Mrs. Lincoln had invited me to accompany her to City Point. I went to the White House, and told her that if she intended to return, I would regard it as a privilege to go with her, as City Point was near Petersburg, my old home. Mrs. L. said she designed returning, and would be delighted to take me with her; so it was arranged that I should accompany her.

A few days after we were on board the steamer, *en route* for City Point. Mrs. Lincoln was joined by Mrs. Secretary Harlan and daughter, Senator Sumner, and several other gentlemen.

Prior to this, Mr. Lincoln had started for City Point, and before we reached our destination he had visited Richmond, Petersburg, and other points. We arrived on Friday, and Mrs. Lincoln was much disappointed when she learned that the President had visited the late Confederate capital, as she had greatly desired to be with him when he entered the conquered stronghold. It was immediately arranged that the entire party on board the River Queen should visit Richmond, and other points, with the President. The next morning, after the arrangement was perfected, we were steaming up James River— the river that so long had been impassable, even to our gunboats. The air was balmy, and the banks of the river were beautiful, and fragrant with the first sweet blossoms of spring. For hours I stood on deck, breathing the pure air, and viewing the landscape on either side of the majestically flowing river. Here stretched fair fields, emblematic of peace—and here deserted camps and frowning forts, speaking of the stern vicissitudes of war. Alas ! how many changes

had taken place since my eye had wandered over
the classic fields of dear old Virginia! A birthplace is always dear, no matter under what circumstances you were born, since it revives in
memory the golden hours of childhood, free from
philosophy, and the warm kiss of a mother. I
wondered if I should catch a glimpse of a familiar face; I wondered what had become of those
I once knew; had they fallen in battle, been
scattered by the relentless tide of war, or were
they still living as they lived when last I saw
them? I wondered, now that Richmond had
fallen, and Virginia been restored to the cluster-
ing stars of the Union, if the people would come
together in the bonds of peace; and as I gazed
and wondered, the River Queen rapidly carried
us to our destination.

The Presidential party were all curiosity on
entering Richmond. They drove about the
streets of the city, and examined every object of
interest. The Capitol presented a desolate ap-

pearance—desks broken, and papers scattered promiscuously in the hurried flight of the Confederate Congress. I picked up a number of papers, and, by curious coincidence, the resolution prohibiting all free colored people from entering the State of Virginia. In the Senate chamber I sat in the chair that Jefferson Davis sometimes occupied; also in the chair of the Vice-President, Alexander H. Stephens. We paid a visit to the mansion occupied by Mr. Davis and family during the war, and the ladies who were in charge of it scowled darkly upon our party as we passed through and inspected the different rooms. After a delightful visit we returned to City Point.

That night, in the cabin of the River Queen, smiling faces gathered around the dinner-table. One of the guests was a young officer attached to the Sanitary Commission. He was seated near Mrs. Lincoln, and, by way of pleasantry, remarked : "Mrs. Lincoln, you should have seen the President the other day, on his triumphal entry into Richmond. He was the cynosure of all eyes. The ladies kissed their hands to him, and greeted him with the waving of handkerchiefs. He is quite a hero when surrounded by pretty young ladies."

The young officer suddenly paused with a look of embarrassment. Mrs. Lincoln turned to him with flashing eyes, with the remark that his familiarity was offensive to her. Quite a scene followed, and I do not think that the Captain who incurred Mrs. Lincoln's displeasure will ever forget that memorable evening in the cabin of the River Queen, at City Point.

Saturday morning the whole party decided to visit Petersburg, and I was only too eager to accompany them.

When we arrived at the city, numbers crowded around the train, and a little ragged negro boy ventured timidly into the car occupied by Mr. Lincoln and immediate friends, and in replying to numerous questions, used the word "tote."

"Tote," remarked Mr. Lincoln; "what do you mean by tote?"

"Why, massa, to tote um on your back."

"Very definite, my son; I presume when you tote a thing, you carry it. By the way, Sumner," turning to the Senator, "what is the origin of tote?"

"Its origin is said to be African. The Latin word *totum*, from *totus*, means all—an entire body—the whole."

"But my young friend here did not mean an entire body, or anything of the kind, when he said he would tote my things for me," interrupted the President.

"Very true," continued the Senator. " He used the word tote in the African sense, to carry, to bear. Tote in this sense is defined in our standard dictionaries as a colloquial word of the Southern States, used especially by the negroes."

"Then you regard the word as a good one?"

"Not elegant, certainly. For myself, I should

prefer a better word; but since it has been established by usage, I cannot refuse to recognize it."

Thus the conversation proceeded in pleasant style.

Getting out of the car, the President and those with him went to visit the forts and other scenes, while I wandered off by myself in search of those whom I had known in other days. War, grim-visaged war, I soon discovered had brought many changes to the city so well known to me in the days of my youth. I found a number of old friends, but the greater portion of the population were strange to me. The scenes suggested painful memories, and I was not sorry to turn my back again upon the city. A large, peculiarly shaped oak tree, I well remember, attracted the particular attention of the President; it grew upon the outskirts of Petersburg, and as he had discovered it on his first visit, a few days previous to the second, he insisted that the party should go with him to take a look at the isolated

8

and magnificent specimen of the stately grandeur
of the forest.   Every member of the party was
only too willing to accede to the President's request, and the visit to the oak was made, and
much enjoyed.

On our return to City Point from Petersburg
the train moved slowly, and the President, observing a terrapin basking in the warm sunshine
on the wayside, had the conductor stop the
train, and one of the brakemen bring the terrapin
in to him.   The movements of the ungainly little
animal seemed to delight him, and he amused
himself with it until we reached James River,
where our steamer lay.   Tad stood near, and
joined in the happy laugh with his father.

For a week the River Queen remained in
James River, anchored the greater portion of the
time at City Point, and a pleasant and memorable week was it to all on board.   During the
whole of this time a yacht lay in the stream
about a quarter of a mile distant, and its peculiar

movements attracted the attention of all on board. General Grant and Mrs. Grant were on our steamer several times, and many distinguished officers of the army also were entertained by the President and his party.

Mr. Lincoln, when not off on an excursion of any kind, lounged about the boat, talking familiarly with every one that approached him.

The day before we started on our journey back to Washington, Mr. Lincoln was engaged in reviewing the troops in camp. He returned to the boat in the evening, with a tired, weary look.

" Mother," he said to his wife, " I have shaken so many hands to-day that my arms ache to-night. I almost wish that I could go to bed now."

As the twilight shadows deepened the lamps were lighted, and the boat was brilliantly illuminated; as it lay in the river, decked with many-colored lights, it looked like an enchanted floating palace. A military band was on board, and as the hours lengthened into night it discoursed sweet music. Many officers came on board to say good-by, and the scene was a brilliant one indeed. About 10 o'clock Mr. Lincoln was called upon to make a speech. Rising to his feet, he said :

"You must excuse me, ladies and gentlemen. I am too tired to speak to-night. On next Tuesday night I make a speech in Washington, at which time you will learn all I have to say. And now, by way of parting from the brave soldiers of our gallant army, I call upon the band to play Dixie. It has always been a favorite of mine, and since we have captured it, we have a perfect right to enjoy it." On taking his seat the band at once struck up with Dixie, that sweet, inspiring air ; and when the music died away, there were clapping of hands and other manifestations of applause.

At 11 o'clock the last good-by was spoken, the

lights were taken down, the River Queen round-
ed out into the water and we were on our
way back to Washington. We arrived at the
Capital at 6 o'clock on Sunday evening, where
the party separated, each going to his and her own
home. This was one of the most delightful trips
of my life, and I always revert to it with feelings
of genuine pleasure.

CHAPTER XI.

The Assassination of President Lincoln.

 HAD never heard Mr. Lincoln make a public speech, and, knowing the man so well, was very anxious to hear him. On the morning of the Tuesday after our return from City Point, Mrs. Lincoln came to my apartments, and before she drove away I asked permission to come to the White House that night and hear Mr. Lincoln speak.

"Certainly, Lizabeth; if you take any interest in political speeches, come and listen in welcome."

"Thank you, Mrs. Lincoln. May I trespass

further on your kindness by asking permission to bring a friend with me ? "

" Yes, bring your friend also. By the way, come in time to dress me before the speaking commences."

"I will be in time. You may rely upon that. Good morning," I added, as she swept from my room, and, passing out into the street, entered her carriage and drove away.

About 7 o'clock that evening I entered the White House. As I went up-stairs I glanced into Mr. Lincoln's room through the half-open door, and seated by a desk was the President, looking over his notes and muttering to himself. His face was thoughtful, his manner abstracted, and I knew, as I paused a moment to watch him, that he was rehearsing the part that he was to play in the great drama soon to commence.

Proceeding to Mrs. Lincoln's apartment, I worked with busy fingers, and in a short time her toilette was completed.

Great crowds began to gather in front of the
White House, and loud calls were made for
the President. The band stopped playing, and
as he advanced to the centre window over the
door to make his address, I looked out, and
never saw such a mass of heads before. It was
like a black, gently swelling sea. The swaying
motion of the crowd, in the dim uncertain light,
was like the rising and falling of billows—like
the ebb and flow of the tide upon the stranded
shore of the ocean. Close to the house the faces
were plainly discernible, but they faded into
mere ghostly outlines on the outskirts of the
assembly; and what added to the weird, spectral
beauty of the scene, was the confused hum of
voices that rose above the sea of forms, sounding
like the subdued, sullen roar of an ocean storm,
or the wind soughing through the dark lonely
forest. It was a grand and imposing scene, and
when the President, with pale face and his soul
flashing through his eyes, advanced to speak, he

looked more like a demi-god than a man crowned with the fleeting days of mortality.

The moment the President appeared at the window he was greeted with a storm of applause, and voices re-echoed the cry, " A light! a light! "

A lamp was brought, and little Tad at once rushed to his father's side, exclaiming:

" Let me hold the light, Papa! let me hold the light! "

Mrs. Lincoln directed that the wish of her son be gratified, and the lamp was transferred to his hands. The father and son standing there in the presence of thousands of free citizens, the one lost in a chain of eloquent ideas, the other looking up into the speaking face with a proud, manly look, formed a beautiful and striking tableau.

There were a number of distinguished gentlemen, as well as ladies, in the room, nearly all of whom remarked the picture.

I stood a short distance from Mr. Lincoln, and as the light from the lamp fell full upon him,

8*

making him stand out boldly in the darkness, a sudden thought struck me, and I whispered to the friend at my side:

"What an easy matter would it be to kill the President, as he stands there! He could be shot down from the crowd, and no one be able to tell who fired the shot."

I do not know what put such an idea into my head, unless it was the sudden remembrance of the many warnings that Mr. Lincoln had received.

The next day, I made mention to Mrs. Lincoln of the idea that had impressed me so strangely the night before, and she replied with a sigh:

"Yes, yes, Mr. Lincoln's life is always exposed. Ah, no one knows what it is to live in constant dread of some fearful tragedy. The President has been warned so often, that I tremble for him on every public occasion. I have a presentiment that he will meet with a sudden and violent end. I pray God to protect my beloved husband from the hands of the assassin."

Mr. Lincoln was fond of pets. He had two goats that knew the sound of his voice, and when he called them they would come bounding to his side. In the warm bright days, he and Tad would sometimes play in the yard with these goats, for an hour at a time. One Saturday afternoon I went to the White House to dress Mrs. Lincoln. I had nearly completed my task when the President came in. It was a bright day, and walking to the window, he looked down into the yard, smiled, and, turning to me, asked :

" Madam Elizabeth, you are fond of pets, are you not ? "

" O yes, sir," I answered.

" Well, come here and look at my two goats. I believe they are the kindest and best goats in the world. See how they sniff the clear air, and skip and play in the sunshine. Whew ! what a jump," he exclaimed as one of the goats made a lofty spring. " Madam Elizabeth, did you ever before see such an active goat ? " Musing a moment, he continued: "He feeds on my bounty, and jumps with joy. Do you think we could call him a bounty-jumper? But I flatter the bounty-jumper. My goat is far above him. I would rather wear his horns and hairy coat through life, than demean myself to the level of the man who plunders the national treasury in the name of patriotism. The man who enlists into the service for a consideration, and deserts the moment he receives his money but to repeat the play, is bad enough; but the men who manipulate the grand machine and who simply make the bounty-jumper their agent in an outrageous fraud are far worse. They are beneath the worms that crawl in the dark hidden places of earth."

His lips curled with haughty scorn, and a cloud was gathering on his brow. Only a moment the shadow rested on his face. Just then both goats looked up at the window and shook their heads as if they would say "How d'ye do, old friend?"

"See, Madam Elizabeth," exclaimed the President in a tone of enthusiasm, "my pets recognize me. How earnestly they look! There they go again; what jolly fun!" and he laughed outright as the goats bounded swiftly to the other side of the yard. Just then Mrs. Lincoln called out, "Come, Lizabeth; if I get ready to go down this evening I must finish dressing myself, or you must stop staring at those silly goats."

Mrs. Lincoln was not fond of pets, and she could not understand how Mr. Lincoln could take so much delight in his goats. After Willie's death, she could not bear the sight of anything he loved, not even a flower. Costly bouquets were presented to her, but she turned from them with a shudder, and either placed them in a room where she could not see them, or threw them out of the window. She gave all of Willie's toys—everything connected with him— away, as she said she could not look upon them without thinking of her poor dead boy, and to think of him, in his white shroud and cold grave, was maddening. I never in my life saw a more peculiarly constituted woman. Search the world over, and you will not find her counterpart. After Mr. Lincoln's death, the goats that he loved so well were given away—I believe to Mrs. Lee, *née* Miss Blair, one of the few ladies with whom Mrs. Lincoln was on intimate terms in Washington.

During my residence in the Capital I made my home with Mr. and Mrs. Walker Lewis, people of my own race, and friends in the truest sense of the word.

The days passed without any incident of particular note disturbing the current of life. On Friday morning, April 14th—alas! what American does not remember the day—I saw Mrs. Lincoln but for a moment. She told me that she was to attend the theatre that night with the President, but I was not summoned to assist her in making her toilette. Sherman had swept from

the northern border of Georgia through the heart
of the Confederacy down to the sea, striking the
death-blow to the rebellion. Grant had pursued
General Lee beyond Richmond, and the army of
Virginia, that had made such stubborn resistance,
was crumbling to pieces. Fort Sumter had
fallen;—the stronghold first wrenched from the
Union, and which had braved the fury of Federal
guns for so many years, was restored to the
Union; the end of the war was near at hand,
and the great pulse of the loyal North thrilled
with joy. The dark war-cloud was fading, and
a white-robed angel seemed to hover in the sky,
whispering " Peace—peace on earth, good-will
toward men ! " Sons, brothers, fathers, friends,
sweethearts were coming home. Soon the white
tents would be folded, the volunteer army be dis-
banded, and tranquillity again reign. Happy,
happy day!—happy at least to those who fought
under the banner of the Union. There was
great rejoicing throughout the North. From the

Atlantic to the Pacific, flags were gayly thrown to the breeze, and at night every city blazed with its tens of thousand lights. But scarcely had the fireworks ceased to play, and the lights been taken down from the windows, when the lightning flashed the most appalling news over the magnetic wires. "The President has been murdered!" spoke the swift-winged messenger, and the loud huzza died upon the lips. A nation suddenly paused in the midst of festivity, and stood paralyzed with horror—transfixed with awe.

Oh, memorable day! Oh, memorable night! Never before was joy so violently contrasted with sorrow.

At 11 o'clock at night I was awakened by an old friend and neighbor, Miss M. Brown, with the startling intelligence that the entire Cabinet had been assassinated, and Mr. Lincoln shot, but not mortally wounded. When I heard the words I felt as if the blood had been frozen in my veins, and that my lungs must collapse for the want of air. Mr. Lincoln shot! the Cabinet assassinated! What could it mean? The streets were alive with wondering, awe-stricken people. Rumors flew thick and fast, and the wildest reports came with every new arrival. The words were repeated with blanched cheeks and quivering lips. I waked Mr. and Mrs. Lewis, and told them that the President was shot, and that I must go to the White House. I could not remain in a state of uncertainty. I felt that the house would not hold me. They tried to quiet me, but gentle words could not calm the wild tempest. They quickly dressed themselves, and we sallied out into the street to drift with the excited throng. We walked rapidly towards the White House, and on our way passed the residence of Secretary Seward, which was surrounded by armed soldiers, keeping back all intruders with the point of the bayonet. We hurried on, and as we approached the White House, saw that it too was surrounded with soldiers. Every entrance was strongly guarded, and no one was permitted to pass. The guard at the gate told us that Mr. Lincoln had not been brought home, but refused to give any other information. More excited than ever, we wandered down the street. Grief and anxiety were making me weak, and as we joined the outskirts of a large crowd, I began to feel as meek and humble as a penitent child. A gray-haired old man was passing. I caught a glimpse of his face, and it seemed so full of kindness and sorrow that I gently touched his arm, and imploringly asked:

"Will you please, sir, to tell me whether Mr. Lincoln is dead or not?"

"Not dead," he replied, "but dying. God help us!" and with a heavy step he passed on.

"Not dead, but dying! then indeed God help us!"

We learned that the President was mortally wounded—that he had been shot down in his box at the theatre, and that he was not expected to live till morning; when we returned home with heavy hearts. I could not sleep. I wanted to go to Mrs. Lincoln, as I pictured her wild with grief; but then I did not know where to find her, and I must wait till morning. Never did the hours drag so slowly. Every moment seemed an age, and I could do nothing but walk about and hold my arms in mental agony.

Morning came at last, and a sad morning was it. The flags that floated so gayly yesterday now were draped in black, and hung in silent folds at half-mast. The President was dead, and a nation was mourning for him. Every house was draped in black, and every face wore a solemn look. People spoke in subdued tones, and glided whisper ingly, wonderingly, silently about the streets.

About eleven o'clock on Saturday morning a carriage drove up to the door, and a messenger asked for "Elizabeth Keckley."

"Who wants her?" I asked.

"I come from Mrs. Lincoln. If you are Mrs.

Keckley, come with me immediately to the White House."

I hastily put on my shawl and bonnet, and was driven at a rapid rate to the White House. Everything about the building was sad and solemn. I was quickly shown to Mrs. Lincoln's room, and on entering, saw Mrs. L. tossing uneasily about upon a bed. The room was darkened, and the only person in it besides the widow of the President was Mrs. Secretary Welles, who had spent the night with her. Bowing to Mrs. Welles, I went to the bedside.

"Why did you not come to me last night, Elizabeth—I sent for you?" Mrs. Lincoln asked in a low whisper.

"I did try to come to you, but I could not find you," I answered, as I laid my hand upon her hot brow.

I afterwards learned, that when she had partially recovered from the first shock of the terrible tragedy in the theatre, Mrs. Welles asked:

" Is there no one, Mrs. Lincoln, that you desire to have with you in this terrible affliction ? "

" Yes, send for Elizabeth Keckley. I want her just as soon as she can be brought here. "

Three messengers, it appears, were successively despatched for me, but all of them mistook the number and failed to find me.

Shortly after entering the room on Saturday morning, Mrs. Welles excused herself, as she said she must go to her own family, and I was left alone with Mrs. Lincoln.

She was nearly exhausted with grief, and when she became a little quiet, I asked and received permission to go into the Guests' Room, where the body of the President lay in state. When I crossed the threshold of the room, I could not help recalling the day on which I had seen little Willie lying in his coffin where the body of his father now lay. I remembered how the President had wept over the pale beautiful face of his gifted boy, and now the President himself was dead. The last time I saw him he spoke kindly to me, but alas! the lips would never move again. The light had faded from his eyes, and when the light went out the soul went with it. What a noble soul was his—noble in all the noble attributes of God! Never did I enter the solemn chamber of death with such palpitating heart and trembling footsteps as I entered it that day. No common mortal had died. The Moses of my people had fallen in the hour of his triumph. Fame had woven her choicest chaplet for his brow. Though the brow was cold and pale in death, the chaplet should not fade, for God had studded it with the glory of the eternal stars.

When I entered the room, the members of the Cabinet and many distinguished officers of the army were grouped around the body of their fallen chief. They made room for me, and, approaching the body, I lifted the white cloth from the white face of the man that I had worshipped as an idol—looked upon as a demi-god. Notwithstanding the violence of the death of the President, there was something beautiful as well as grandly solemn in the expression of the placid face. There lurked the sweetness and gentleness of childhood, and the stately grandeur of godlike intellect. I gazed long at the face, and turned away with tears in my eyes and a choking sensation in my throat. Ah! never was man so widely mourned before. The whole world bowed their heads in grief when Abraham Lincoln died.

Returning to Mrs. Lincoln's room, I found her in a new paroxysm of grief. Robert was bending over his mother with tender affection, and little Tad was crouched at the foot of the bed with a world of agony in his young face. I shall never forget the scene—the wails of a broken heart, the unearthly shrieks, the terrible convulsions, the wild, tempestuous outbursts of grief from the soul. I bathed Mrs. Lincoln's nead with cold water, and soothed the terrible tornado as best I could. Tad's grief at his father's death was as great as the grief of his mother, but her terrible outbursts awed the boy into silence. Sometimes he would throw his arms around her neck, and exclaim, between his broken sobs, " Don't cry so, Mamma! don't cry, or you will make me cry, too! You will break my heart."

Mrs. Lincoln could not bear to hear Tad cry, and when he would plead to her not to break his heart, she would calm herself with a great effort, and clasp her child in her arms.

Every room in the White House was darkened, and every one spoke in subdued tones, and moved about with muffled tread. The very atmosphere breathed of the great sorrow which weighed heavily upon each heart. Mrs. Lincoln never left her room, and while the body of her husband was being borne in solemn state from the Atlantic to the broad prairies of the West, she was weeping with her fatherless children in her private chamber. She denied admittance to almost every one, and I was her only companion, except her children, in the days of her great sorrow.

There were many surmises as to who was implicated with J. Wilkes Booth in the assassination of the President. A new messenger had accompanied Mr. and Mrs. Lincoln to the theatre on that terrible Friday night. It was the duty of this messenger to stand at the door of the box during the performance, and thus guard the inmates from all intrusion. It appears that the messenger was carried away by the play, and so neglected his duty that Booth gained easy admission to the box. Mrs. Lincoln firmly believed that this messenger was implicated in the assassination plot.

One night I was lying on a lounge near the bed occupied by Mrs. Lincoln. One of the servants entering the room, Mrs. L. asked:

" Who is on watch to-night ? "

" The new messenger," was the reply.

"What! the man who attended us to the theatre on the night my dear, good husband was murdered! He, I believe, is one of the murderers. Tell him to come in to me."

The messenger had overheard Mrs. Lincoln's words through the half-open door, and when he came in he was trembling violently.

She turned to him fiercely: "So you are on guard to-night—on guard in the White House after helping to murder the President!"

"Pardon me, but I did not help to murder the President. I could never stoop to murder—much less to the murder of so good and great a man as the President."

"But it appears that you *did* stoop to murder."

"No, no! don't say that," he broke in. "God knows that I am innocent."

"I don't believe you. Why were you not at the door to keep the assassin out when he rushed into the box?"

"I did wrong, I admit, and I have bitterly repented it, but I did not help to kill the President. I did not believe that any one would try to kill so good a man in such a public place, and the belief made me careless. I was attracted by the play, and did not see the assassin enter the box."

"But you should have seen him. You had no business to be careless. I shall always believe that you are guilty. Hush! I shan't hear another word," she exclaimed, as the messenger essayed to reply. "Go now and keep your watch," she added, with an imperious wave of her hand. With mechanical step and white face the messenger left the room, and Mrs. Lincoln fell back on her pillow, covered her face with her hands, and commenced sobbing.

Robert was very tender to his mother in the days of her sorrow.

He suffered deeply, as his haggard face indicated, but he was ever manly and collected when in the presence of his mother. Mrs. Lincoln was extremely nervous, and she refused to have anybody about her but myself.   Many ladies called, but she received none of them.   Had she been less secluded in her grief, perhaps she would have had many warmer friends to-day than she has. But far be it from me to harshly judge the sorrow of any one.   Could the ladies who called to condole with Mrs. Lincoln, after the death of her husband, and who were denied admittance to her chamber, have seen how completely prostrated she was with grief, they would have learned to speak more kindly of her.   Often at night, when Tad would hear her sobbing, he would get up, and come to her bed in his white sleeping-clothes : " Don't cry, Mamma; I cannot sleep if you cry !   Papa was good, and he has gone to heaven.   He is happy there.   He is with God and brother Willie.   Don't cry, Mamma, or I will cry too."

The closing appeal always proved the most effectual, as Mrs. Lincoln could not bear to hear her child cry.

Tad had been petted by his father, but petting could not spoil such a manly nature as his. He seemed to realize that he was the son of a President—to realize it in its loftiest and noblest sense. One morning, while being dressed, he looked up at his nurse, and said : " Pa is dead. I can hardly believe that I shall never see him again. I must learn to take care of myself now." He looked thoughtful a moment, then added, " Yes, Pa is dead, and I am only Tad Lincoln now, little Tad, like other little boys. I am not a President's son now. I won't have many presents any more. Well, I will try and be a good boy, and will hope to go some day to Pa and brother Willie, in heaven." He was a brave, manly child, and knew that influence had passed out of their hands with the death of his father, and that his position in life was altered. He seemed to feel that people petted him, and gave him presents, because they wanted to please the President of the United States. From that period forward he became more independent, and in a short time learned to dispense with the services of a nurse. While in Chicago, I saw him get out his clothes one Sunday morning and dress himself, and the change was such a great one to me —for while in the White House, servants obeyed his every nod and bid—that I could scarcely refrain from shedding tears. Had his father lived, I knew it would have been different with his favorite boy. Tad roomed with Robert, and he always took pride in pleasing his brother.

After the Committee had started West with the body of the President, there was quite a breeze of excitement for a few days as to where the remains should be interred. Secretary Stanton and others held frequent conferences with Robert, Mr. Todd, Mrs. Lincoln's cousin, and Dr. Henry, an old schoolmate and friend of Mr. Lincoln. The city authorities of Springfield had purchased a beautiful plat of ground in a prosperous portion of the city, and work was rapidly progressing on the tomb, when Mrs. Lincoln made strenuous objection to the location. She declared that she would stop the body in Chicago before it should be laid to rest in the lot purchased for the purpose by the City of Springfield. She gave as a reason, that it was her desire to be laid by the side of her husband when she died, and that such would be out of the question in a public place of the kind. As is well known, the difficulty was finally settled by placing the remains of the President in the family vault at Oak Ridge, a charming spot for the home of the dead.

After the President's funeral Mrs. Lincoln rallied, and began to make preparations to leave the White House. One day she suddenly exclaimed: "God, Elizabeth, what a change! Did ever woman have to suffer so much and experience so great a change? I had an ambition to be Mrs. President; that ambition has been gratified, and now I must step down from the pedestal. My poor husband! had he never been President, he might be living to-day. Alas! all is over with me!"

Folding her arms for a few moments, she rocked back and forth, then commenced again, more vehemently than ever: "My God, Elizabeth, I can never go back to Springfield! no, never, until I go in my shroud to be laid by my dear husband's side, and may Heaven speed that day! I should like to live for my sons, but life is so full of misery that I would rather die." And then she would go off into a fit of hysterics.

CHAPTER XII.

OR five weeks Mrs. Lincoln was con-
fined to her room. Packing afford-
ed quite a relief, as it so closely
occupied us that we had not much
time for lamentation.

Letters of condolence were received from all
parts of the country, and even from foreign po-
tentates, but Mr. Andrew Johnson, the successor
of Mr. Lincoln, never called on the widow, or
even so much as wrote a line expressing sympathy
for her grief and the loss of her husband. Robert called on him one day to tell him that his
mother would turn the White House over to him

in a few days, and he never even so much as inquired after their welfare. Mrs. Lincoln firmly believes that Mr. Johnson was concerned in the assassination plot.

In packing, Mrs. Lincoln gave away everything intimately connected with the President, as she said that she could not bear to be reminded of the past. The articles were given to those who were regarded as the warmest of Mr. Lincoln's admirers. All of the presents passed through my hands. The dress that Mrs. Lincoln wore on the night of the assassination was given to Mrs. Slade, the wife of an old and faithful messenger. The cloak, stained with the President's blood, was given to me, as also was the bonnet worn on the same memorable night. Afterwards I received the comb and brush that Mr. Lincoln used during his residence at the White House. With this same comb and brush I had often combed his head. When almost ready to go down to a reception, he would turn to me with a quizzical look : " Well, Madam Elizabeth, will you brush my bristles down to-night ? "

" Yes, Mr. Lincoln."

Then he would take his seat in an easy-chair, and sit quietly while I arranged his hair. As may well be imagined, I was only too glad to accept this comb and brush from the hands of Mrs. Lincoln. The cloak, bonnet, comb, and brush, the glove worn at the first reception after the second inaugural, and Mr. Lincoln's over-shoes, also given to me, I have since donated for the benefit of Wilberforce University, a colored college near Xenia, Ohio, destroyed by fire on the night that the President was murdered.

There was much surmise, when Mrs. Lincoln left the White House, what her fifty or sixty boxes, not to count her score of trunks, could contain. Had the government not been so liberal in furnishing the boxes, it is possible that there would have been less demand for so much transportation. The boxes were loosely packed, and many of them with articles not worth carrying away. Mrs. Lincoln had a passion for hoarding old things, believing, with Toodles, that they were " handy to have about the house."

The bonnets that she brought with her from Springfield, in addition to every one purchased during her residence in Washington, were packed in the boxes, and transported to Chicago. She remarked that she might find use for the material some day, and it was prudent to look to the future. I am sorry to say that Mrs. Lincoln's foresight in regard to the future was only confined to cast-off clothing, as she owed, at the time of the President's death, different store bills amounting to seventy thousand dollars. Mr. Lincoln knew nothing of these bills, and the only happy feature of his assassination was that he died in ignorance of them. Had he known to what extent his wife was involved, the fact would have embittered the only pleasant moments of his life. I disclose this secret in regard to Mrs. Lincoln's debts, in order to explain why she should subsequently have labored under pecuniary embarrassment. The children, as well as herself, had received a vast number of presents during Mr. Lincoln's administration, and these presents constituted a large item in the contents of the boxes. The only article of furniture, so far as I know, taken away from the White House by Mrs. Lincoln, was a little dressing-stand used by the President. I recollect hearing him say one day:

"Mother, this little stand is so handy, and suits me so well, that I do not know how I shall get along without it when we move away from here." He was standing before a mirror, brushing his hair, when he made the remark.

"Well, father," Mrs. Lincoln replied, "if you like the stand so well, we will take it with us when we go away."

"Not for the world," he exclaimed; but she interrupted him:

"I should like to know what difference it makes if we put a better one in its place."

"That alters the question. If you will put a stand in its place worth twice as much as this one, and the Commissioner consents, then I have no objection."

Mrs. Lincoln remembered these words, and, with the consent of the Commissioner, took the stand to Chicago with her for the benefit of little Tad. Another stand, I must not forget to add, was put in its place.

It is charged that a great deal of furniture was lost from the White House during Mr. Lincoln's occupation of it. Very true, and it can be accounted for in this way: In some respects, to put the case very plainly, Mrs. Lincoln was "penny wise and pound foolish." When she moved into the White House, she discharged the Steward, whose business it was to look after the affairs of the household. When the Steward was dismissed, there was no one to superintend affairs, and the servants carried away many pieces of furniture. In this manner the furniture rapidly disappeared.

Robert was frequently in the room where the boxes were being packed, and he tried without avail to influence his mother to set fire to her vast stores of old goods. "What are you going to do with that old dress, mother?" he would ask.

"Never mind, Robert, I will find use for it. You do not understand this business."

"And what is more, I hope I never may understand it. I wish to heaven the car would take fire in which you place these boxes for transportation to Chicago, and burn all of your old plunder up;" and then, with an impatient gesture, he would turn on his heel and leave the room.

"Robert is so impetuous," his mother would say to me, after the closing of the door. "He never thinks about the future. Well, I hope that he will get over his boyish notions in time."

Many of the articles that Mrs. Lincoln took away from the White House were given, after her arrival in Chicago, for the benefit of charity fairs.

At last everything was packed, and the day for departure for the West came. I can never forget that day; it was so unlike the day when the body of the President was borne from the hall in grand and solemn state. Then thousands gathered to bow the head in reverence as the plumed hearse drove down the line. There was all the pomp of. military display—drooping flags, battalions with reversed arms, and bands playing dirge-like airs. Now, the wife of the President was leaving the White House, and there was scarcely a friend to tell her good-by. She passed down the public stairway, entered her carriage, and quietly drove to the depot where we took the cars. The silence was almost painful.

It had been arranged that I should go to

Chicago. When Mrs. Lincoln first suggested her plan, I strongly objected; but I had been with her so long, that she had acquired great power over me.

"I cannot go West with you, Mrs. Lincoln," I said, when the idea was first advanced.

"But you must go to Chicago with me, Elizabeth; I cannot do without you."

"You forget my business, Mrs. Lincoln. I cannot leave it. Just now I have the spring trousseau to make for Mrs. Douglas, and I have promised to have it done in less than a week."

"Never mind. Mrs. Douglas can get some one else to make her trousseau. You may find it to your interest to go. I am very poor now, but if Congress makes an appropriation for my benefit, you shall be well rewarded."

"It is not the reward, but—" I commenced, by way of reply, but she stopped me:

"Now don't say another word about it, if you do not wish to distress me. I have determined that you shall go to Chicago with me, and you *must* go."

When Mrs. Douglas learned that Mrs. Lincoln wished me to accompany her West, she sent me word:

"Never mind me. Do all you can for Mrs. Lincoln. My heart's sympathy is with her."

Finding that no excuse would be accepted, I made preparations to go to Chicago with Mrs. L.

The green car had specially been chartered for us, and in this we were conveyed to the West. Dr. Henry accompanied us, and he was remarkably attentive and kind. The first night out, Mrs. Lincoln had a severe headache; and while I was bathing her temples, she said to me:

"Lizabeth, you are my best and kindest friend, and I love you as my best friend. I wish it were in my power to make you comfortable for the balance of your days. If Congress provides for me, depend upon it, I will provide for you."

The trip was devoid of interest. We arrived

in Chicago without accident or delay, and apartments were secured for us at the Tremont House, where we remained one week. At the expiration of this time Mrs. Lincoln decided that living at the hotel was attended with too much expense, so it was arranged that we should go to the country. Rooms were selected at Hyde Park, a summer resort.

Robert and Tad accompanied their mother to Hyde Park. We arrived about 3 o'clock in the afternoon of Saturday. The place had just been opened the summer before, and there was a newness about everything. The accommodations were not first-class, the rooms being small and plainly furnished. It was a lively day for us all. Robert occupied himself unpacking his books, and arranging them on the shelves in the corner of his small but neat room. I assisted him, he talking pleasantly all the while. When we were through, he folded his arms, stood off a little distance from the mantel, with an abstracted look as if he were thinking of the great change in his fortunes—contrasting the present with the past. Turning to me, he asked: "Well, Mrs. Keckley, how do you like our new quarters?"

"This is a delightful place, and I think you will pass your time pleasantly," I answered.

He looked at me with a quizzical smile, then remarked: "You call it a delightful place! Well, perhaps it is. Since you do not have to stay here, you can safely say as much about the charming situation as you please. I presume that I must put up with it, as mother's pleasure must be consulted before my own. But candidly, I would almost as soon be dead as be compelled to remain three months in this dreary house."

He seemed to feel what he said, and going to the window, he looked out upon the view with moody countenance. I passed into Mrs. Lincoln's room, and found her lying upon the bed, sobbing as if her heart would break.

"What a dreary place, Lizzie! and to think

that I should be compelled to live here, because I have not the means to live elsewhere. Ah! what a sad change has come to us all." I had listened to her sobbing for eight weeks, therefore I was never surprised to find her in tears. Tad was the only cheerful one of the party. He was a child of sunshine, and nothing seemed to dampen the ardor of his spirits.

Sunday was a very quiet day. I looked out of my window in the morning, upon the beautiful lake that formed one of the most delightful views from the house. The wind was just strong enough to ripple the broad bosom of the water, and each ripple caught a jewel from the sunshine, and threw it sparkling up towards the sky. Here and there a sail-boat silently glided into view, or sank below the faint blue line that marked the horizon—glided and melted away like the spectral shadows that sometimes haunt the white snow-fields in the cold, tranquil light of a winter's moon. As I stood by my window that morning, looking out upon the lake, my thoughts were etherealized—the reflected sunbeams suggested visions of crowns studded with the jewels of eternal life and I wondered how any one could call Hyde Park a dreary place. I had seen so much trouble in my life, that I was willing to fold my arms and sink into a passive slumber—slumber anywhere, so the great longing of the soul was gratified—rest.

Robert spent the day in his room with his books, while I remained in Mrs. Lincoln's room, talking with her, contrasting the present with the past, and drawing plans for the future. She held no communication, by letter or otherwise, with any of her relatives or old friends, saying that she wished to lead a secluded life for the summer. Old faces, she claimed, would only bring back memories of scenes that she desired to forget ; and new faces, she felt assured, could not sympathize with her distress, or add to the comforts of her situation.

On Monday morning, Robert was getting ready to ride into Chicago, as business called him to the city.

"Where you goin', brother Bob?"—Tad generally called Robert, brother Bob.

"Only into town!" was the brief reply.

"Mayn't I go with you?"

"Ask mother. I think that she will say no."

Just then Mrs. Lincoln came in, and Tad ran to her, with the eager question:

"Oh, Ma! can't I go to town with brother Bob? I want to go so badly."

"Go to town! No; you must stay and keep me company. Besides, I have determined that you shall get a lesson every day, and I am going to commence to-day with you."

"I don't want to get a lesson—I won't get a lesson," broke in the impetuous boy. "I don't want to learn my book; I want to go to town!"

"I suppose you want to grow up to be a great dunce. Hush, Tad; you shall not go to town until you have said a lesson;" and the mother looked resolute.

"May I go after I learn my book?" was the next question.

"Yes; if Robert will wait for you."

"Oh, Bob will wait; won't you, Bob?"

"No, I cannot wait; but the landlord is going in this afternoon, and you can go with him. You must do as mother tells you, Tad. You are getting to be a big boy now, and must start to school next fall; and you would not like to go to school without knowing how to read."

"Where's my book, Ma? Get my book quick. I will say my lesson," and he jumped about the room, boisterously, boy-like.

"Be quiet, Tad. Here is your book, and we will now begin the first lesson," said his mother, as she seated herself in an easy-chair.

Tad had always been much humored by his parents, especially by his father. He suffered from a slight impediment in his speech, and had never been made to go to school; consequently his book knowledge was very limited. I knew that his education had been neglected, but had no idea he was so deficient as the first lesson at Hyde Park proved him to be.

Drawing a low chair to his mother's side, he opened his book, and began to slowly spell the first word, "A-p-e."

"Well, what does A-p-e spell?"

"Monkey," was the instant rejoinder. The word was illustrated by a small wood-cut of an ape, which looked to Tad's eyes very much like a monkey; and his pronunciation was guided by the picture, and not by the sounds of the different letters.

"Nonsense!" exclaimed his mother. "A-p-e does not spell monkey."

"Does spell monkey! Isn't that a monkey?" and Tad pointed triumphantly to the picture.

"No, it is not a monkey."

"Not a monkey! what is it, then?"

"An ape."

"An ape! 'taint an ape. Don't I know a monkey when I see it?"

"No, if you say that is a monkey."

"I do know a monkey. I've seen lots of them in the street with the organs. I know a monkey better than you do, 'cause I always go out into the street to see them when they come by, and you don't."

"But, Tad, listen to me. An ape is a species of the monkey. It looks like a monkey, but it is not a monkey."

"It shouldn't look like a monkey, then. Here, Yib"—he always called me Yib—"isn't this a monkey, and don't A-p-e spell monkey? Ma don't know anything about it;" and he thrust his book into my face in an earnest, excited manner.

I could not longer restrain myself, and burst out laughing. Tad looked very much offended, and I hastened to say: "I beg your pardon,

Master Tad; I hope that you will excuse my want of politeness."

He bowed his head in a patronizing way, and returned to the original question: "Isn't this a monkey? Don't A-p-e spell monkey?"

"No, Tad; your mother is right. A-p-e spells ape."

"You don't know as much as Ma. Both of you don't know anything;" and Master Tad's eyes flashed with indignation.

Robert entered the room, and the question was referred to him. After many explanations, he succeeded in convincing Tad that A-p-e does not spell monkey, and the balance of the lesson was got over with less difficulty.

Whenever I think of this incident I am tempted to laugh; and then it occurs to me that had Tad been a negro boy, not the son of a President, and so difficult to instruct, he would have been called thick-skulled, and would have been held up as an example of the inferiority of race.

I know many full negro boys, able to read and write, who are not older than Tad Lincoln was when he persisted that A-p-c spelt monkey. Do not imagine that I desire to reflect upon the intellect of little Tad. Not at all; he is a bright boy, a son that will do honor to the genius and greatness of his father; I only mean to say that some incidents are about as damaging to one side of the question as to the other. If a colored boy appears dull, so does a white boy sometimes; and if a whole race is judged by a single example of apparent dulness, another race should be judged by a similar example.

I returned to Washington, with Mrs. Lincoln's best wishes for my success in business. The journey was devoid of incident. After resting a few days, I called at the White House, and transacted some business for Mrs. Lincoln. I had no desire to enter the house, for everything about it bitterly reminded me of the past; and when I came out of the door, I hoped that I had crossed the threshold for the last time. I was asked by some of my friends if I had sent my business cards to Mr. Johnson's family, and my answer was that I had not, as I had no desire to work for the President's family. Mr. Johnson was no friend to Mr. Lincoln, and he had failed to treat Mrs. Lincoln, in the hour of her greatest sorrow, with even common courtesy.

Having promised to make a spring trousseau for Mrs. Senator Douglas as soon as I should return from Chicago, I called on her to meet the engagement. She appeared pleased to see me, and in greeting me, asked, with evident surprise:

" Why, Keckley "—she always called me Keckley—" is this you? I did not know you were coming back. It was reported that you designed remaining with Mrs. Lincoln all summer."

" Mrs. Lincoln would have been glad to have kept me with her had she been able."

" Able! What do you mean by that?"

" Simply this: Already she is laboring under pe-

cuniary embarrassment, and was only able to pay
my expenses, and allow me nothing for my time."

"You surprise me. I thought she was left in
good circumstances."

"So many think, it appears. Mrs. Lincoln, I
assure you, is now practising the closest economy.
I must do something for myself, Mrs. Douglas, so I
have come back to Washington to open my shop."

The next day I collected my assistants, and
my business went on as usual. Orders came in
more rapidly than I could fill them. One day, in
the middle of the month of June, the girl who
was attending the door came into the cutting-
room, where I was hard at work :

"Mrs. Keckley, there is a lady below, who
wants to see you."

"Who is she?"

"I don't know. I did not learn her name."

"Is her face familiar? Does she look like a
regular customer?"

"No, she is a stranger. I don't think she was

ever here before.   She came in an open carriage, with a black woman for an attendant."

" It may be the wife of one of Johnson's new secretaries. Do go down, Mrs. Keckley," exclaimed my work-girls in a chorus. I went below, and on entering the parlor, a plainly dressed lady rose to her feet, and asked :

" Is this the dressmaker ? "

" Yes, I am a dressmaker."

" Mrs. Keckley ? "

" Yes."

" Mrs. Lincoln's former dressmaker, were you not ? "

" Yes, I worked for Mrs. Lincoln."

" Are you very busy now ? "

" Very, indeed."

" Can you do anything for me ? "

" That depends upon what is to be done, and when it is to be done."

" Well, say one dress now, and several others a few weeks later."

"I can make one dress for you now, but no more. I cannot finish the one for you in less than three weeks."

"That will answer. I am Mrs. Patterson, the daughter of President Johnson. I expect my sister, Mrs. Stover, here in three weeks, and the dress is for her. We are both the same size, and you can fit the dress to me."

The terms were satisfactorily arranged, and after measuring Mrs. Patterson, she bade me good morning, entered her carriage, and drove away.

When I went up-stairs into the work-room, the girls were anxious to learn who my visitor was.

"It was Mrs. Patterson, the daughter of President Johnson," I answered, in response to several questions.

"What! the daughter of our good Moses. Are you going to work for her?"

"I have taken her order."

"I fear that Johnson will prove a poor Moses, and I would not work for any of the family," remarked one of the girls. None of them ap-peared to like Mr. Lincoln's successor.

I finished the dress for Mrs. Patterson, and it gave satisfaction. I afterwards learned that both Mrs. Patterson and Mrs. Stover were kind-hearted, plain, unassuming women, making no pretensions to elegance. One day when I called at the White House, in relation to some work that I was doing for them, I found Mrs. Patter-son busily at work with a sewing-machine. The sight was a novel one to me for the White House, for as long as I remained with Mrs. Lincoln, I do not recollect ever having seen her with a needle in her hand. The last work done for the Johnsons by me were two dresses, one for each of the sisters. Mrs. Patterson subsequently wrote me a note, requesting me to cut and fit a dress for her; to which I replied that I never cut and fitted work to be made up outside of my work-room. This brought our business relations to an abrupt end.

The months passed, and my business prospered.

I continually received letters from Mrs. Lincoln, and as the anniversary of her husband's death approached, she wrote in a sadder strain. Before I left Chicago she had exacted the promise that should Congress make an appropriation for her benefit, I must join her in the West, and go with her to visit the tomb of the President for the first time. The appropriation was made one of the conditions of my visit, for without relief from Congress she would be unable to bear my expenses. The appropriation was not made; and so I was unable to join Mrs. Lincoln at the appointed time. She wrote me that her plan was to leave Chicago in the morning with Tad, reach Springfield at night, stop at one of the hotels, drive out to Oak Ridge the next day, and take the train for Chicago the same evening, thus avoiding a meeting with any of her old friends. This plan, as she afterwards wrote me, was carried out. When the second anniversary approached, President Johnson and party were "swinging round the circle," and as they were to visit Chicago, she was especially anxious to be away from the city when they should arrive; accordingly she hurried off to Springfield, and spent the time in weeping over the tomb where repose the hallowed ashes of her husband.

During all this time I was asked many questions about Mrs. Lincoln, some prompted by friendship, but a greater number by curiosity; but my brief answers, I fear, were not always accepted as the most satisfactory.

CHAPTER XIII.

The Origin of the Rivalry between Mr. Douglas and Mr. Lincoln.

RS. LINCOLN from her girlhood up had an ambition to become the wife of a President. When a little girl, as I was told by one of her sisters, she was disposed to be a little noisy at times, and was self-willed. One day she was romping about the room, making more noise than the nerves of her grandmother could stand. The old lady looked over her spectacles, and said, in a commanding tone :

"Sit down, Mary. Do be quiet. What on

earth do you suppose will become of you if you go on this way ? "

" Oh, I will be the wife of a President some day," carelessly answered the petted child.

Mrs. Lincoln, as Miss Mary Todd, was quite a belle in Springfield, Illinois, and from all accounts she was fond of flirting. She generally managed to keep a half-dozen gentlemen biting at the hook that she baited so temptingly for them. The world, if I mistake not, are not aware that the rivalry between Mr. Lincoln and Mr. Stephen A. Douglas commenced over the hand of Miss Mary Todd. The young lady was ambitious, and she smiled more sweetly upon Mr. Douglas and Mr. Lincoln than any of her other admirers, as they were regarded as rising men. She played her part so well that neither of the rivals for a long time could tell who would win the day. Mr. Douglas first proposed for her hand, and she discarded him. The young man urged his suit boldly :

"Mary, you do not know what you are refusing. You have always had an ambition to become the wife of a President of the United States. Pardon the egotism, but I fear that in refusing my hand to-night you have thrown away your best chance to ever rule in the White House."

"I do not understand you, Mr. Douglas."

"Then I will speak more plainly. You know, Mary, that I am ambitious like yourself, and something seems to whisper in my ear, 'You will be President some day.' Depend upon it, I shall make a stubborn fight to win the proud position."

"You have my best wishes, Mr. Douglas; still I cannot consent to be your wife. I shall become Mrs. President, or I am the victim of false prophets, but it will not be as Mrs. Douglas."

I have this little chapter in a romantic history from the lips of Mrs. Lincoln herself.

At one of the receptions at the White House, shortly after the first inauguration, Mrs. Lincoln joined in the promenade with Senator Douglas. He was holding a bouquet that had been presented to her, and as they moved along he said:

"Mary, it reminds me of old times to have you lean upon my arm."

"You refer to the days of our youth. I must do you the credit, Mr. Douglas, to say, that you were a gallant beau."

"Not only a beau, but a lover. Do you remember the night our flirtation was brought to an end?"

"Distinctly. You now see that I was right. I am Mrs. President, but not Mrs. Douglas."

"True, you have reached the goal before me, but I do not despair. Mrs. Douglas—a nobler woman does not live—if I am spared, may possibly succeed you as Mrs. President."

A few evenings after Mr. Douglas had been discarded, Mr. Lincoln made a formal proposal for the hand of Miss Todd, but it appears that the young lady was not willing to capitulate at once. She believed that she could send her lover adrift to-day and win him back to-morrow.

"You are bold, Mr. Lincoln."

"Love makes me bold."

"You honor me, pardon me, but I cannot consent to be your wife."

"Is this your final answer, Miss Todd?" and the suitor rose nervously to his feet.

"I do not often jest, Mr. Lincoln. Why should I reconsider to-morrow my decision of to-day."

"Excuse me. Your answer is sufficient. I was led to hope that I might become dearer to you than a friend, but the hope, it seems, has proved an idle one. I have the honor to say good night, Miss Todd," and pale, yet calm, Mr. Lincoln bowed himself out of the room.

He rushed to his office in a frantic state of mind. Dr. Henry, his most intimate friend, happened to come in, and was surprised to see the young lawyer walking the floor in an agitated manner.

"What is the matter, Lincoln? You look desperate."

"Matter! I am sick of the world. It is a heartless, deceitful world, and I care not how soon I am out of it."

"You rave. What has happened? Have you been quarrelling with your sweetheart?"

"Quarrel! I wish to God it was a quarrel, for then I could look forward to reconciliation; the girl has refused to become my wife, after leading me to believe that she loved me. She is a heartless coquette."

"Don't give up the conquest so easily. Cheer up, man, you may succeed yet. Perhaps she is only testing your love."

"No! I believe that she is going to marry Douglas. If she does I will blow my brains out."

"Nonsense! That would not mend matters.

Your brains were given to you for different use. Come, we will go to your room now. Go to bed and sleep on the question, and you will get up feeling stronger to-morrow;" and Dr. Henry took the arm of his friend Lincoln, led him home, and saw him safely in bed.

The next morning the doctor called at Mr. Lincoln's room, and found that his friend had passed a restless night. Excitement had brought on fever, which threatened to assume a violent form, as the cause of the excitement still remained. Several days passed, and Mr. Lincoln was confined to his bed. Dr. Henry at once determined to call on Miss Todd, and find out how desperate the case was. Miss Todd was glad to see him, and she was deeply distressed to learn that Mr. Lincoln was ill. She wished to go to him at once, but the Doctor reminded her that she was the cause of his illness. She frankly acknowledged her folly, saying that she only desired to test the sincerity of Mr. Lincoln's love, that he was the idol of her heart, and that she would become his wife.

The Doctor returned with joyful news to his patient. The intelligence proved the best remedy for the disease. Mutual explanations followed, and in a few months Mr. Lincoln led Miss Todd to the altar in triumph.

I learned these facts from Dr. Henry and Mrs. Lincoln. I believe them to be facts, and as such have recorded them. They do not agree with Mr. Herndon's story, that Mr. Lincoln never loved but one woman, and that woman was Ann Rutledge; but then Mr. Herndon's story must be looked upon as a pleasant piece of fiction. When it appeared, Mrs. Lincoln felt shocked that one who pretended to be the friend of her dead husband should deliberately seek to blacken his memory. Mr. Lincoln was far too honest a man to marry a woman that he did not love. He was a kind and an indulgent husband, and when he saw faults in his wife he excused them as he would excuse the impulsive acts of a child. In fact, Mrs. Lincoln was never more pleased than when the President called her his child-wife.

Before closing this rambling chapter I desire to refer to another incident.

After the death of my son, Miss Mary Welsh, a dear friend, one of my old St. Louis patrons, called to see me, and on broaching the cause of my grief, she condoled with me. She knew that I had looked forward to the day when my son would be a support to me—knew that he was to become the prop and main-stay of my old age, and knowing this, she advised me to apply for a pension. I disliked the idea very much, and told her so— told her that I did not want to make money out of his death. She explained away all of my objections—argued that Congress had made an appropriation for the specific purpose of giving a pension to every widow who should lose an only son in the war, and insisted that I should have my rights. She was so enthusiastic in the matter that she went to see Hon. Owen Lovejoy, then a member of the House from Illinois, and laid my case before him. Mr. Lovejoy was very kind, and said as I was entitled to the pension, I should have it, even if he had to bring the subject before Congress. I did not desire public agitation, and Mr. Lovejoy prepared my claim and laid it before the Commissioners. In the meantime he left Washington, and Mr. Joseph Lovejoy, his brother, prosecuted the claim for me, and finally succeeded in securing me a pension of eight dollars per month. Mr. Joseph Lovejoy was inclined to the Democratic party, and he pressed my claim with great earnestness; he hoped that the claim would not be allowed, as he said the rejection of it would make capital for his party. Nevertheless the pension was granted, and I am none the less thankful to Mr. Joseph Lovejoy for his kindness to me, and interest in my welfare.

11

CHAPTER XIV.

OLD FRIENDS.

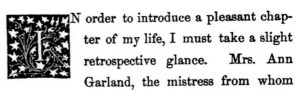N order to introduce a pleasant chapter of my life, I must take a slight retrospective glance. Mrs. Ann Garland, the mistress from whom I purchased my freedom in St. Louis, had five daughters, all lovely, attractive girls. I used to take pride in dressing the two eldest, Miss Mary and Miss Carrie, for parties. Though the family labored under pecuniary embarrassment, I worked for these two young girls, and they were always able to present a good appearance in society. They were much admired, and both

made the best matches of the season. Miss
Mary married Dr. Pappan, and Miss Carrie, Dr.
John Farrow. I loved them both tenderly, and
they were warmly attached to me. Both are
now dead, and when the death-film was gathering in the eyes, each called for me and asked to
die in my arms. Miss Carrie did not long sur-
vive her sister, and I wept many tears over the
death-beds of the two lovely flowers that had
blossomed so sweetly beneath my eyes. Each
breathed her last in the arms that had sheltered
them so often in the bright rosy period of life.
My mother took care of my son, and Miss
Nannie Garland, the fourth daughter, when a
wee thing, became my especial charge. She
slept in my bed, and I watched over her as if
she had been my own child. She called me
Yiddie, and I could not have loved her more
tenderly had she been the sister of my unfortunate boy. She was about twelve years old
when I purchased my freedom, and resigned my

charge to other hands. After Mr. Garland's
death, the widow moved to Vicksburg, Mississippi, and I lost sight of the family for a few
years. My mother accompanied them to Vicksburg, where she died. I made two visits to
Vicksburg as a free woman, the object of my
second visit being to look after the few effects
left by my mother. As I did not visit my
mother's grave at the time, the Garlands were
much surprised, but I offered no explanation.
The reason is not difficult to understand. My
mother was buried in a public ground, and the
marks of her grave, as I learned, were so obscure
that the spot could not be readily designated.
To look upon a grave, and not feel certain whose
ashes repose beneath the sod, is painful, and the
doubt which mystifies you, weakens the force, if
not the purity, of the love-offering from the heart.
Memory preserved a sunny picture of my mother's face, and I did not wish to weave sombre
threads—threads suggestive of a deserted grave-

yard—into it, and thus impair its beauty. After spending a few weeks with the family, I returned to St. Louis, and then came North. The war broke out, and I lost all trace of the Garlands. Often, during my residence in Washington, I recalled the past, and wondered what had become of those who claimed my first duty and my first love. When I would mention their names and express interest in their welfare, my Northern friends would roll up their eyes in surprise.

"Why, Lizzie, how can you have a kind thought for those who inflicted a terrible wrong upon you by keeping you in bondage?" they would ask.

"You forget the past is dear to every one, for to the past belongs that golden period, the days of childhood. The past is a mirror that reflects the chief incidents of my life. To surrender it is to surrender the greatest part of my existence— early impressions, friends, and the graves of my father, my mother, and my son. These people are associated with everything that memory holds dear, and so long as memory proves faithful, it is but natural that I should sigh to see them once more."

"But they have forgotten you. They are too selfish to give a single thought to you, now that you no longer are their slave."

"Perhaps so, but I cannot believe it. You do not know the Southern people as well as I do— how warm is the attachment between master and slave."

My Northern friends could not understand the feeling, therefore explanation was next to useless. They would listen with impatience, and remark at the close, with a shrug of the shoulders, "You have some strange notions, Lizzie."

In the fall of 1865 a lady called on me at my apartments in Washington. Her face looked familiar, but I could not place her. When I entered the room, she came towards me eagerly:

"You are surprised to see me, I know. I am

just from Lynchburg, and when I left cousin Ann I promised to call and see you if I came to Washington. I am here, you see, according to promise."

I was more bewildered than ever.

"Cousin Ann! Pardon me—"

"Oh, I see you do not recognize me. I am Mrs. General Longstreet, but you knew me when a girl as Bettie Garland."

"Bettie Garland! And is this indeed you? I am *so* glad to see you. Where does Miss Ann live now?" I always called my last mistress, Miss Ann.

"Ah! I thought you could not forget old friends. Cousin Ann is living in Lynchburg. All the family are in Virginia. They moved to the old State during the war. Fannie is dead. Nannie has grown into a woman and is married to General Meem. Hugh was killed in the war, and now only Spot, Maggie, and Nannie are left."

" Fannie, dead! and poor Hugh! You bring sad news as well as pleasant. And so my little pet is married? I can hardly believe it; she was only a child when I saw her last."

" Yes, Nannie is married to a noble man. General Meem belongs to one of the best families in Virginia. They are now living at Rude's Hill, up beyond Winchester, in the Shenandoah Valley. All of them want to see you very badly."

" I should be delighted to go to them. Miss Bettie, I can hardly realize that you are the wife of General Longstreet; and just think, you are now sitting in the very chair and the very room where Mrs. Lincoln has often sat!"

She laughed: "The change is a great one, Lizzie; we little dream to-day what to-morrow will bring forth. Well, we must take a philosophical view of life. After fighting so long against the Yankees, General Longstreet is now in Washington, sueing for pardon, and we propose to live in peace with the United States again."

I had many questions to ask her about old friends, and the time passed rapidly. She greeted me with the frankness that she had always extended to me, and I was transported to days of the long-ago. Her stay in Washington was brief, as the General arranged his business, and they left the capital the next day.

Mrs. Longstreet gave me the Garlands' address, and I wrote to them, expressing the hope that I would be able to see them before long. In reply came letters full of tender sympathy and affection. In the winter of 1865, Miss Nannie wrote to me that she had the best husband in the world; that they designed going to housekeeping in the spring, and that they would be glad to have me make them a visit in July, 1866. She sent me a pressing invitation. "You must come to me, dear Lizzie," she wrote. "We are now living at Rude's Hill. I am dying to see you. Ma, Maggie, Spot, and Minnie, sister Mary's child, are with me, and you only are needed to

11*

make the circle complete. Come; I will not take no for an answer."

I was anxious to go myself, and when I received the urgent invitation I concluded to go at once, and I wrote them to expect me in August. On the 10th of August I left Washington for Virginia, taking the train for Harper's Ferry. The journey was attended with several disappointments. We arrived at Harper's Ferry in the night, and being asleep at the time, I was carried to the station beyond, where I had to wait and take the return train. After returning to Harper's Ferry, where I changed cars for Winchester, I missed the train, and was detained another day. From Winchester the only way to reach Rude's Hill was by a line of stages. We commenced the weary drive in the evening, and rode all night. A young gentleman in the stage said that he knew General Meem well, and that he would tell me when we reached the place. Relying upon him, I went to sleep, and it appears that the polite young gentleman followed my example. About four o'clock in the morning one of the passengers shook me, and asked:

"Aunty, don't you want to get out at Rude's Hill?"

I started up, rubbing my eyes. "Yes. Are we there?"

"More than there. We have passed it."

"Passed it!"

"Yes. It is six miles back. You should not sleep so soundly, Aunty."

"Why *did* you not tell me sooner? I am *so* anxious to be there."

"Fact is, I forgot it. Never mind. Get out at this village, and you can find conveyance back."

The village, New Market, was in a dilapidated condition; everything about it spoke plainly of the sad destruction of war. Getting out of the stage I went into a house, by courtesy named a hotel, where I obtained a cup of coffee.

" Is there no conveyance from here to Rude's Hill ? " I asked.

" Yes; the stage returns this evening," answered the landlord.

" This evening ! I want to go as soon as possible. I should die if I had to stay all day in this lonely place."

A colored man behind the bar, seeing how earnest I was, came forward, and informed me that he would drive me over to General Meem's place in an hour. This was joyful news, and I urged him to get ready to start as soon as possible.

While standing in the door of the hotel, impatiently waiting for my colored friend to drive round with his little wagon, a fat old lady waddled across the street and greeted me.

" Ain't you Lizzie ? "

" Yes," I answered, surprised that she should know my name.

" I thought so. They have been expecting you

at Rude's Hill every day for two weeks, and they do but little but talk about you. Mrs. Meem was in town yesterday, and she said that she expected you this week certain. They will be mighty glad to see you. Why, will you believe it! they actually have kept a light burning in the front window every night for ten nights, in order that you might not go by the place should you arrive in the night."

"Thank you. It is pleasant to know that I am expected. I fell asleep in the stage, and failed to see the light, so am here instead of at Rude's Hill."

Just then the colored man drove up with the wagon, and I got in with him, and was soon on the road to General Meem's country-seat.

As we drove up to Rude's Hill, I observed a young man standing in the yard, and believing it to be Spot, whom I had not seen for eight years, I beckoned to him. With an exclamation of joy, he came running towards me. His movements attracted the attention of the family, and in a minute the door was crowded with anxious, inquiring faces. "It is Lizzie! It is Lizzie!" was the happy cry from all parties. In my eagerness to get to them, I stepped from the wagon to the top of the stile, intending to make a triumphant leap into the yard; but, alas! my exultation was brief. My hoop-skirt caught on one of the posts, and I fell sprawling into the yard. Spot reached me first and picked me up, only to put me into the arms of Miss Nannie, her sister Maggie, and Mrs. Garland. Could my friends of the North have seen that meeting, they would never have doubted again that the mistress had any affection for her former slave. I was carried to the house in triumph. In the parlor I was divested of my things, and placed in an easy-chair before a bright fire. The servants looked on in amazement.

"Lizzie, you are not changed a bit. You look as young as when you left us in St. Louis, years ago," and Mrs. Meem, my foster child, kissed me again.

"Here, Lizzie, this is Minnie, Minnie Pappan, sister Mary's child. Hasn't she grown?" and Miss Maggie led a tall, queenly lady up to me.

"Minnie! Poor dear Miss Mary's child! I can hardly believe it. She was only a baby when I saw her last. It makes me feel old to see how large she has grown. Miss Minnie, you are larger than your mother was—your dear mother whom I held in my arms when she died;" and I brushed a tear from each of my eyes.

"Have you had your breakfast, Lizzie?" asked Mrs. Garland.

"No, she has not," exclaimed her children in a chorus. "I will get her breakfast for her," and Nannie, Maggie, and Minnie started for the kitchen.

"It is not necessary that all should go," said Mrs. Garland. "Here is the cook, she will get breakfast ready."

But the three did not heed her. All rushed to the kitchen, and soon brought me a nice hot breakfast.

While I was eating, the cook remarked: "I declar, I nebber did see people carry on so. Wonder if I should go off and stay two or three years, if all ob you wud hug and kiss me so when I cum back?"

After I had finished my breakfast, General Meem came in. He greeted me warmly. "Lizzie, I am very glad to see you. I feel that you are an old acquaintance, I have heard so much of you through my wife, her sister, and her mother. Welcome to Rude's Hill."

I was much pleased with his appearance, and closer acquaintance proved him to be a model gentleman.

Rude's Hill, during the war, was once occupied by General Stonewall Jackson for his head-quarters, which gave more than ordinary interest to the place. The location was delightful, but the

marks of war could be seen everywhere on the
plantation.   General Meem was engaged in
planting, and he employed a large number of servants to assist him in his work.   About a mile
from Rude's Hill was Mount Airy, the elegant
country-seat of the General's brother.   The two
families visited each other a great deal, and as
both entertained plenty of company, the Autumn
months passed pleasantly.   I was comfortably
quartered at Rude's Hill, and was shown every
attention.   We sewed together, talking of old
times, and every day either drove out, or rode on
horseback.   The room in which I sat in the day-
time was the room that General Jackson always
slept in, and people came from far and near to
look at it.   General Jackson was the ideal soldier
of the Southern people, and they worshipped him
as an idol.   Every visitor would tear a splinter
from the walls or windows of the room, to take
away and treasure as a priceless relic.

It did not take me long to discover that I was

an object of great curiosity in the neighborhood. My association with Mrs. Lincoln, and my attachment for the Garlands, whose slave I had once been, clothed me with romantic interest.

Colonel Harry Gilmore, well known as a partisan leader in Maryland and Virginia during the war, was a frequent visitor at Mount Airy and Rude's Hill. One day I accompanied a party to a tournament, and General Meem laughed pleasantly over the change that had come to me in so short a time.

" Why, Lizzie, you are riding with Colonel Gilmore. Just think of the change from Lincoln to Gilmore! It sounds like a dream. But then the change is an evidence of the peaceful feeling of this country; a change, I trust, that augurs brighter days for us all."

I had many long talks with Mrs. Garland, in one of which I asked what had become of the only sister of my mother, formerly maid to Mrs. G.'s mother.

"She is dead, Lizzie. Has been dead for some years. A maid in the old time meant something different from what we understand by a maid at the present time. Your aunt used to scrub the floor and milk a cow now and then, as well as attend to the orders of my mother. My mother was severe with her slaves in some respects, but then her heart was full of kindness. She had your aunt punished one day, and not liking her sorrowful look, she made two extravagant promises in order to effect a reconciliation, both of which were accepted. On condition that her maid would look cheerful, and be good and friendly with her, the mistress told her she might go to church the following Sunday, and that she would give her a silk dress to wear on the occasion. Now my mother had but one silk dress in the world, silk not being so plenty in those days as it is now, and yet she gave this dress to her maid to make friends with her. Two weeks afterward mother was sent for to spend the day at a neighbor's house, and on inspecting her wardrobe, discovered that she had no dress fit to wear in company. She had but one alternative, and that was to appeal to the generosity of your aunt Charlotte. Charlotte was summoned, and enlightened in regard to the situation ; the maid proffered to loan the silk dress to her mistress for the occasion, and the mistress was only too glad to accept. She made her appearance at the social gathering, duly arrayed in the silk that her maid had worn to church on the preceding Sunday."

We laughed over the incident, when Mrs. Garland said : "Lizzie, during the entire war I used to think of you every day, and have longed to see you so much. When we heard you were with Mrs. Lincoln, the people used to tell me that I was foolish to think of ever seeing you again—that your head must be completely turned. But I knew your heart, and could not believe that you would forget us. I always argued that you would come and see us some day."

"You judged me rightly, Miss Ann. How could I forget you whom I had grown up with from infancy. Northern people used to tell me that you would forget me, but I told them I knew better, and hoped on."

"Ah! love is too strong to be blown away like gossamer threads. The chain is strong enough to bind life even to the world beyond the grave. Do you always feel kindly towards me, Lizzie?"

"To tell you candidly, Miss Ann, I have but one unkind thought, and that is, that you did not give me the advantages of a good education. What I have learned has been the study of after years."

"You are right. I did not look at things then as I do now. I have always regretted that you were not educated when a girl. But you have not suffered much on this score, since you get along in the world better than we who enjoyed every educational advantage in childhood."

I remained five weeks at Rude's Hill, and

they were five of the most delightful weeks of my life. I designed going direct to Richmond, but the cholera was reported to be raging in that city, so I took the train for Baltimore. In Baltimore I stopped with Mrs. Annette Jordan. Mrs. Garland had given me a letter to Mrs. Douglas Gordon, who introduced me to several Baltimore ladies, among others Mrs. Doctor Thomas, who said to me, with tears in her eyes: "Lizzie, you deserve to meet with success for having been so kind to our friends in the days of the past. I wish there were more women in the world like you. I will always do what little I can to promote your welfare."

After remaining in Baltimore a few days, I came to the conclusion that I could do better in Washington; so I returned to the capital, and re-opened my business.

In the spring of 1867, Miss Maggie Garland paid a visit to Baltimore. Before leaving Virginia she said to some of her friends in Lynchburg that she designed going by Washington to see Lizzie. Her friends ridiculed the idea, but she persisted:

"I love Lizzie next to mother. She has been a mother to us all. Half the pleasure of my visit is that I will be able to see her."

She wrote me a letter, saying that she designed visiting me, asking if it would be agreeable. I replied, "Yes, come by all means. I shall be *so* glad to see you."

She came and stayed at my rooms, and expressed surprise to find me so comfortably fixed.

I cannot do better than conclude this chapter with two letters from my dear young friends, the first from Mrs. General Meem, and the second from Miss Maggie Garland. These letters show the goodness of their hearts and the frankness of their natures. I trust that they will not object to the publicity that I give them:

"RUDE'S HILL, Sept. 14, 1867.

"MY DEAR LIZZIE :—I am nearly ashamed of myself for neglecting to acknowledge the receipt of your letter, and the very acceptable box of patterns, some weeks ago ; but you will pardon my remissness, I know, for you can imagine what a busy time I've had all summer, with a house full of company most of the time, and with very inefficient servants, and in some departments *none at all ;* so I have had to be at times dining-room servant, house-maid, and the last and most difficult, dairy-maid. But I have turned that department over to our gardener, who, though as green at the business as myself, seems willing to learn, and has been doing the milking all summer. These are a *few* of the reasons why I have not written to you before, for I hope you will always believe that you occupy a large place in my memory and affection, whether I write to you or not ; and such a poor correspondent as yourself ought not to complain. Mother, Mag, Uncle

John, and Spot are still with us ; the former will
pass the winter with me, but the others all talk
of leaving before long. The approach of winter
always scatters our guests, and we have to spend
the long, dreary winters alone. But we are to
have the railroad to Mt. Jackson by Christmas,
perhaps sooner ; and then, if we can raise the
wind, we can spend a portion of the winter in the
city, and I hope you will find time to come up
and *spend the day* with me, as we will be near
neighbors. I so seldom indulge in the pleasant
task of writing letters that I scarcely know what
will interest my correspondent, but I flatter myself that *you* will be glad to hear anything and
everything about us all, so I'll begin with the
children. Hugh has improved a great deal, and
is acknowledged to be the smartest child and the
finest looking in the State ; he talks as plainly as
I do, and just as understandingly as a child of
ten years old ; his nurse often says we need not
set our hearts on that child, he is too smart ever

to be raised; but I trust his *badness* will save him, for he is terribly spoilt, as such interesting children are bound to be. Miss Eliza, no longer called *Jane,* is getting to be a little 'star girl,' as her Papa calls her; she is just learning to walk, and says a good many words quite plainly. You would never take her for the same little *cry-baby* of last summer, and she is a little beauty too—as white as the driven snow, with the most beautiful blue eyes, and long, dark lashes you ever saw. She will set *somebody* crazy if she grows up to be as lovely as she now promises to be. My dear good husband has been, like myself, run to death this summer; but it agrees with him, and I never saw him looking better. He has fallen off a little, which is a great improvement, I think. He often speaks of you, and wonders if you were sufficiently pleased with your visit last summer to repeat it. I hope so, for we will always be glad to welcome you to Rude's Hill, whenever you have time to come;

provided, of course, you have the wish also. Spot expects to hang out his shingle in St. Louis next winter. His health is greatly improved, though he is still very thin, and very, very much like dear father. Mag has promised to teach a little cousin of ours, who lives in Nelson County, until February, and will leave here in two weeks to commence her labors. I hate to see her leave, but she is bent on it, and our winters are so unattractive that I do not like to insist on her shutting herself up all winter with three old people. She will have very pleasant society at Cousin Buller's, and will perhaps spend the rest of the winter with Aunt Pris, if Uncle Armistead remains in Binghampton, New York, as he talks of doing. Do write to me before you get too busy with your fall and winter work; I am so anxious to hear all your plans, and about your stay in New York. By the by, I will have to direct this to Washington, as I do not know your New York address. I suppose your friends will forward it. If you are going to remain any length of time in New York, send me your address, and I will write again.   *   *

I have somehow made out a long letter, though there is not much in it, and I hope you will do the same before long. *All* send love.

                "Yours affectionately,
                        "N. R. G. MEEM.

"My pen and ink are both so wretched that I fear you will find some difficulty in making out this scratch; but *put on your specks*, and what you can't read, just guess at. I enclose a very poor likeness of Hugh taken last spring; don't show it to anybody, for I assure you there is scarcely the faintest resemblance to him now in it.

                        "N. R. G. M."

I give only a few extracts from the pleasant letter from Miss Maggie Garland. The reader will observe that she signs herself "Your child, Mag," an expression of love warmly appreciated by me:

"So many months have passed, my dear Lizzie, since I was cheered by a sight of your welcome handwriting, that I must find out what is the matter, and see if I can't persuade you to write me a few lines. Whatever comes, ' weal or woe,' you know I shall always love you, and I have no idea of letting you forget me; so just make up your mind to write me a nice long letter, and tell me what you are doing with yourself this cold weather. I am buried in the wilds of Amherst, and the cold, chilling blasts of December come whistling around, and tell us plainly that the reign of the snow-king has begun in good earnest. Since October I have been teaching for my cousin, Mr. Claiborne, and although I am very happy, and every one is so kind to me, I shall not be sorry when the day comes when I shall shut up school-books forever. None of 'Miss Ann's' children were cut out for 'school-marms,' were they, Yiddie? I am sure I was only made to ride in my carriage, and play on the piano. Don't you think so? * * * You must write me where you are, so I can stop and see you on my way North; for you know, dear Lizzie, no one can take your place in my heart. I expect to spend the Christmas holidays in Lynchburg. It will be very gay there, and I will be glad enough to take a good dance. This is a short letter to send you after such a long silence, but 'tis too cold to write. Let me hear from you very soon.

"Your child MAG.

"Please write, for I long to hear from you."

CHAPTER XV.

The Secret History of Mrs. Lincoln's Wardrobe in New York.

N March, 1867, Mrs. Lincoln wrote to me from Chicago that, as her income was insufficient to meet her expenses, she would be obliged to give up her house in the city, and return to boarding. She said that she had struggled long enough to keep up appearances, and that the mask must be thrown aside. "I have not the means," she wrote, "to meet the expenses of even a first-class boarding-house, and must sell out and secure cheap rooms at some place in the country.

It will not be startling news to you, my dear Lizzie, to learn that I must sell a portion of my wardrobe to add to my resources, so as to enable me to live decently, for you remember what I told you in Washington, as well as what you understood before you left me here in Chicago. I cannot live on $1,700 a year, and as I have many costly things which I shall never wear, I might as well turn them into money, and thus add to my income, and make my circumstances easier. It is humiliating to be placed in such a position, but, as I am in the position, I must extricate myself as best I can. Now, Lizzie, I want to ask a favor of you. It is imperative that I should do something for my relief, and I want you to meet me in New York, between the 30th of August and the 5th of September next, to assist me in disposing of a portion of my wardrobe."

I knew that Mrs. Lincoln's income was small, and also knew that she had many valuable dresses, which could be of no value to her, packed away in boxes and trunks. I was confident that she would never wear the dresses again, and thought that, since her need was urgent, it would be well enough to dispose of them quietly, and believed that New York was the best place to transact a delicate business of the kind. She was the wife of Abraham Lincoln, the man who had done so much for my race, and I could refuse to do nothing for her, calculated to advance her interests. I consented to render Mrs. Lincoln all the assistance in my power, and many letters passed between us in regard to the best way to proceed. It was finally arranged that I should meet her in New York about the middle of September. While thinking over this question, I remembered an incident of the White House. When we were packing up to leave Washington for Chicago, she said to me, one morning:

"Lizzie, I may see the day when I shall be obliged to sell a portion of my wardrobe. If

Congress does not do something for me, then my dresses some day may have to go to bring food into my mouth, and the mouths of my children."

I also remembered of Mrs. L. having said to me at different times, in the years of 1863 and '4, that her expensive dresses might prove of great assistance to her some day.

"In what way, Mrs. Lincoln? I do not understand," I ejaculated, the first time she made the remark to me.

"Very simple to understand. Mr. Lincoln is so generous that he will not save anything from his salary, and I expect that we will leave the White House poorer than when we came into it; and should such be the case, I will have no further need for an expensive wardrobe, and it will be policy to sell it off."

I thought at the time that Mrs. Lincoln was borrowing trouble from the future, and little dreamed that the event which she so dimly foreshadowed would ever come to pass.

I closed my business about the 10th of September, and made every arrangement to leave Washington on the mission proposed. On the 15th of September I received a letter from Mrs. Lincoln, post-marked Chicago, saying that she should leave the city so as to reach New York on the night of the 17th, and directing me to precede her to the metropolis, and secure rooms for her at the St. Denis Hotel in the name of Mrs. Clarke, as her visit was to be *incog*. The contents of the letter were startling to me. I had never heard of the St. Denis, and therefore presumed that it could not be a first-class house. And I could not understand why Mrs. Lincoln should travel, without protection, under an assumed name. I knew that it would be impossible for me to engage rooms at a strange hotel for a person whom the proprietors knew nothing about. I could not write to Mrs. Lincoln, since she would be on the road to New York before a letter could possibly reach Chicago. I could not telegraph her, for the business was of too delicate a character to be trusted to the wires that would whisper the secret to every curious operator along the line. In my embarrassment, I caught at a slender thread of hope, and tried to derive consolation from it. I knew Mrs. Lincoln to be indecisive about some things, and I hoped that she might change her mind in regard to the strange programme proposed, and at the last moment despatch me to this effect. The 16th, and then the 17th of September passed, and no despatch reached me, so on the 18th I made all haste to take the train for New York. After an anxious ride, I reached the city in the evening, and when I stood alone in the streets of the great metropolis, my heart sank within me. I was in an embarrassing situation, and scarcely knew how to act. I did not know where the St. Denis Hotel was, and was not certain that I should find Mrs. Lincoln there after I should go to it. I walked up to Broadway, and got into a stage

going up town, with the intention of keeping a
close look-out for the hotel in question. A kind-
looking gentleman occupied the seat next to me,
and I ventured to inquire of him :

"If you please, sir, can you tell me where the
St. Denis Hotel is ? "

"Yes; we ride past it in the stage. I will
point it out to you when we come to it."

"Thank you, sir."

The stage rattled up the street, and after a
while the gentleman looked out of the window
and said :

"This is the St. Denis. Do you wish to get
out here ? "

"Thank you. Yes, sir."

He pulled the strap, and the next minute I was
standing on the pavement. I pulled a bell at the
ladies' entrance to the hotel, and a boy coming to
the door, I asked :

"Is a lady by the name of Mrs. Clarke stop-
ping here ? She came last night, I believe."
    12*

"I do not know. I will ask at the office;" and I was left alone.

The boy came back and said:

"Yes, Mrs. Clarke is here. Do you want to see her?"

"Yes."

"Well, just walk round there. She is down here now."

I did not know where "round there" exactly was, but I concluded to go forward.

I stopped, however, thinking that the lady might be in the parlor with company; and pulling out a card, asked the boy to take it to her. She heard me talking, and came into the hall to see herself.

"My dear Lizzie, I am so glad to see you," she exclaimed, coming forward and giving me her hand. "I have just received your note"—I had written her that I should join her on the 18th—"and have been trying to get a room for you. Your note has been here all day, but it was never delivered until to-night. Come in here, until I find out about your room ; " and she led me into the office.

The clerk, like all modern hotel clerks, was exquisitely arrayed, highly perfumed, and too self-important to be obliging, or even courteous.

" This is the woman I told you about. I want a good room for her," Mrs. Lincoln said to the clerk.

" We have no room for her, madam," was the pointed rejoinder.

" But she must have a room. She is a friend of mine, and I want a room for her adjoining mine."

" We have no room for her on your floor."

" That is strange, sir. I tell you that she is a friend of mine, and I am sure you could not give a room to a more worthy person."

" Friend of yours, or not, I tell you we have no room for her on your floor. I can find a place for her on the fifth floor."

" That, sir, I presume, will be a vast improvement on my room. Well, if she goes to the fifth floor, I shall go too, sir. What is good enough for her is good enough for me."

"Very well, madam. Shall I give you adjoining rooms, and send your baggage up?"

"Yes, and have it done in a hurry. Let the boy show us up. Come, Elizabeth," and Mrs. L. turned from the clerk with a haughty glance, and we commenced climbing the stairs. I thought we should never reach the top; and when we did reach the fifth story, what accommodations! Little three-cornered rooms, scantily furnished. I never expected to see the widow of President Lincoln in such dingy, humble quarters.

"How provoking!" Mrs. Lincoln exclaimed, sitting down on a chair when we had reached the top, and panting from the effects of the climbing. "I declare, I never saw such unaccommodating people. Just to think of them sticking us away up here in the attic. I will give them a regular going over in the morning."

"But you forget. They do not know you. Mrs. Lincoln would be treated differently from Mrs. Clarke."

"True, I do forget. Well, I suppose I shall have to put up with the annoyances. Why did you not come to me yesterday, Lizzie? I was almost crazy when I reached here last night, and found you had not arrived. I sat down and wrote you a note—I felt so badly—imploring you to come to me immediately."

This note was afterwards sent to me from Washington. It reads as follows:

"St. Denis Hotel, Broadway, N. Y.
"Wednesday, Sept. 17th.

"My dear Lizzie :—I arrived *here* last evening in utter despair *at not* finding you. I am frightened to death, being here alone. Come, I pray you, by *next* train. Inquire for

"Mrs. Clarke,
" *Room* 94, 5*th or* 6*th Story.*

"House so crowded could not get another spot. I wrote you especially to meet me here last evening; it makes me wild to think of being here alone. Come by *next train*, without fail.

"Your friend,

"Mrs. Lincoln.

"I am booked Mrs. Clarke; inquire for *no other person. Come, come, come.* I will pay your expenses when you arrive here. I shall not leave here or change my room until you come.

"Your friend, M. L.

"Do not leave this house without seeing me.

"*Come !.*"

I transcribe the letter literally.

In reply to Mrs. Lincoln's last question, I explained what has already been explained to the reader, that I was in hope she would change her mind, and knew that it would be impossible to secure the rooms requested for a person unknown to the proprietors or attachés of the hotel.

The explanation seemed to satisfy her. Turning to me suddenly, she exclaimed:

"You have not had your dinner, Lizzie, and must be hungry. I nearly forgot about it in the joy of seeing you. You must go down to the table right away."

She pulled the bell-rope, and a servant appearing, she ordered him to give me my dinner. I followed him down-stairs, and he led me into the dining-hall, and seated me at a table in one corner of the room. I was giving my order, when the steward came forward and gruffly said:

"You are in the wrong room."

"I was brought here by the waiter," I replied.

"It makes no difference; I will find you another place where you can eat your dinner."

I got up from the table and followed him, and when outside of the door, said to him:

"It is very strange that you should permit me to be seated at the table in the dining-room only for the sake of ordering me to leave it the next moment."

"Are you not Mrs. Clarke's servant?" was his abrupt question.

"I am with Mrs. Clarke."

"It is all the same; servants are not allowed to eat in the large dining-room. Here, this way; you must take your dinner in the servants' hall."

Hungry and humiliated as I was, I was willing to follow to any place to get my dinner, for I had been riding all day, and had not tasted a mouthful since early morning.

On reaching the servants' hall we found the door of the room locked. The waiter left me standing in the passage while he went to inform the clerk of the fact.

In a few minutes the obsequious clerk came blustering down the hall:

"Did you come out of the street, or from Mrs. Clarke's room?"

"From Mrs. Clarke's room," I meekly answer

ed. My gentle words seemed to quiet him, and then he explained :

"It is after the regular hour for dinner. The room is locked up, and Annie has gone out with the key."

My pride would not let me stand longer in the hall.

"Very well," I remarked, as I began climbing the stairs, " I will tell Mrs. Clarke that I cannot get any dinner."

He looked after me, with a scowl on his face :

" You need not put on airs ! I understand the whole thing."

I said nothing, but continued to climb the stairs, thinking to myself: " Well, if you understand the whole thing, it is strange that you should put the widow of ex-President Abraham Lincoln in a three-cornered room in the attic of this miserable hotel."

When I reached Mrs. Lincoln's rooms, tears of humiliation and vexation were in my eyes.

"What is the matter, Lizzie?" she asked.

"I cannot get any dinner."

"Cannot get any dinner! What do you mean?"

I then told her of all that had transpired below.

"The insolent, overbearing people!" she fiercely exclaimed. "Never mind, Lizzie, you shall have your dinner. Put on your bonnet and shawl."

"What for?"

"What for! Why, we will go out of the hotel, and get you something to eat where they know how to behave decently;" and Mrs. Lincoln already was tying the strings of her bonnet before the glass.

Her impulsiveness alarmed me.

"Surely, Mrs. Lincoln, you do not intend to go out on the street to-night?"

"Yes I do. Do you suppose I am going to have you starve, when we can find something to eat on every corner?"

"But you forget. You are here as Mrs. Clarke and not as Mrs. Lincoln. You came alone, and the people already suspect that everything is not right. If you go outside of the hotel to-night, they will accept the fact as evidence against you."

"Nonsense; what do you suppose I care for what these low-bred people think? Put on your things."

"No, Mrs. Lincoln, I shall not go outside of the hotel to-night, for I realize your situation, if you do not. Mrs. Lincoln has no reason to care what these people may say about her as Mrs. Lincoln, but she should be prudent, and give them no opportunity to say anything about her as Mrs. Clarke."

It was with difficulty I could convince her that she should act with caution. She was so frank and impulsive that she never once thought that her actions might be misconstrued. It did not occur to her that she might order dinner to be served in my room, so I went to bed without a mouthful to eat.

The next morning Mrs. Lincoln knocked at my door before six o'clock:

" Come, Elizabeth, get up, I know you must be hungry. Dress yourself quickly and we will go out and get some breakfast. I was unable to sleep last night for thinking of you being forced to go to bed without anything to eat."

I dressed myself as quickly as I could, and together we went out and took breakfast, at a restaurant on Broadway, some place between 609 and the St. Denis Hotel. I do not give the number, as I prefer leaving it to conjecture. Of one thing I am certain—the proprietor of the restaurant little dreamed who one of his guests was that morning.

After breakfast we walked up Broadway, and entering Union Square Park, took a seat on one of the benches under the trees, watched the children at play, and talked over the situation.

Mrs. Lincoln told me: "Lizzie, yesterday morning I called for the *Herald* at the breakfast table, and on looking over the list of diamond brokers advertised, I selected the firm of W. H. Brady & Co., 609 Broadway. After breakfast I walked down to the house, and tried to sell them a lot of jewelry. I gave my name as Mrs. Clarke. I first saw Mr. Judd, a member of the firm, a very pleasant gentleman. We were unable to agree about the price. He went back into the office, where a stout gentleman was seated at the desk, but I could not hear what he said. [I know now what was said, and so shall the reader, in parentheses. Mr. Brady has since told me that he remarked to Mr. Judd that the woman must be crazy to ask such outrageous prices, and to get rid of her as soon as possible.] Soon after Mr. Judd came back to the counter, another gentleman, Mr. Keyes, as I have since learned, a silent partner in the house, entered the store. He came to the counter, and in looking over my jewelry discovered my name inside of one of the rings. I had forgotten the ring, and when I saw him looking at the name so earnestly, I snatched the bauble from him and put it into my pocket. I hastily gathered up my jewelry, and started out. They asked for my address, and I left my card, Mrs. Clarke, at the St. Denis Hotel. They are to call to see me this forenoon, when I shall enter into negotiations with them."

Scarcely had we returned to the hotel when Mr. Keyes called, and Mrs. Clarke disclosed to him that she was Mrs. Lincoln. He was much elated to find his surmise correct. Mrs. L. exhibited to him a large number of shawls, dresses, and fine laces, and told him that she was compelled to sell them in order to live. He was an earnest Republican, was much affected by her story, and denounced the ingratitude of the government in the severest terms. She complained to him of the treatment she had received at the St. Denis, and he advised her to move to another hotel forthwith.

She readily consented, and as she wanted to be in an out-of-the-way place where she would not be recognized by any of her old friends, he recommended the Earle Hotel in Canal street.

On the way down to the hotel that morning she acceded to a suggestion made by me, and supported by Mr. Keyes, that she confide in the landlord, and give him her name without registering, so as to ensure the proper respect. Unfortunately, the Earle Hotel was full, and we had to select another place. We drove to the Union Place Hotel, where we secured rooms for Mrs. Clarke, Mrs. Lincoln changing her mind, deeming it would not be prudent to disclose her real name to any one. After we had become settled in our new quarters, Messrs. Keyes and Brady called frequently on Mrs. Lincoln, and held long conferences with her. They advised her to pursue the course she did, and were sanguine of success. Mrs. Lincoln was very anxious to dispose of her things, and return to Chicago as quickly and quietly as possible; but they presented the case in a different light, and, I regret to say, she was guided by their counsel. " Pooh," said Mr. Brady, " place your affairs in our hands, and we will raise you at least $100,000 in a few weeks. The people will not permit the widow of Abraham Lincoln to suffer; they will come to her rescue when they know she is in want."

The argument seemed plausible, and Mrs. Lincoln quietly acceded to the proposals of Keyes and Brady.

We remained quietly at the Union Place Hotel for a few days. On Sunday Mrs. Lincoln accepted the use of a private carriage, and accompanied by me, she drove out to Central Park. We did not enjoy the ride much, as the carriage was a close one, and we could not throw open the window for fear of being recognized by some one of the many thousands in the Park. Mrs. Lincoln wore a heavy veil so as to more effectually conceal her face. We came near being run into, and we had a spasm of alarm, for an accident would have exposed us to public gaze, and of course the masquerade would have been at an end.   On Tuesday I hunted up a number of dealers in second-hand clothing, and had them call at the hotel by appointment.   Mrs. Lincoln soon discovered that they were hard people to drive a bargain with, so on Thursday we got into a close carriage, taking a bundle of dresses and shawls with us, and drove to a number of stores on Seventh Avenue, where an attempt was made to dispose of a portion of the wardrobe.   The dealers wanted the goods for little or nothing, and we found it a hard matter to drive a bargain with them.   Mrs. Lincoln met the dealers squarely, but all of her tact and shrewdness failed to accomplish much. I do not care to dwell upon this portion of my story.   Let it answer to say, that we returned to the hotel more disgusted than ever with the business in which we were engaged.   There was much curiosity at the hotel in relation to us, as our

13

movements were watched, and we were regarded
with suspicion. Our trunks in the main hall
below were examined daily, and curiosity was
more keenly excited when the argus-eyed reporters for the press traced Mrs. Lincoln's name on
the cover of one of her trunks. The letters had
been rubbed out, but the faint outlines remained,
and these outlines only served to stimulate curiosity. Messrs. Keyes and Brady called often,
and they made Mrs. Lincoln believe that, if she
would write certain letters for them to show to
prominent politicians, they could raise a large
sum of money for her. They argued that the
Republican party would never permit it to be
said that the wife of Abraham Lincoln was in
want; that the leaders of the party would make
heavy advances rather than have it published to
the world that Mrs. Lincoln's poverty compelled
her to sell her wardrobe. Mrs. L.'s wants were
urgent, as she had to borrow $600 from Keyes
and Brady, and she was willing to adopt any

scheme which promised to place a good bank account to her credit. At different times in her room at the Union Place Hotel she wrote the following letters:

"CHICAGO, Sept. 18, 1867.

"MR. BRADY, *Commission Broker, No.* 609 *Broadway, New York:*

"I have this day sent to you personal property, which I am compelled to part with, and which you will find of considerable value. The articles consist of four camels' hair shawls, one lace dress and shawl, a parasol cover, a diamond ring, two dress patterns, some furs, etc.

"Please have them appraised, and confer by letter with me. Very respectfully,

"MRS. LINCOLN."

"CHICAGO, ————.

"MR. BRADY, *No.* 609 *Broadway, N. Y. City:*

"* * * * DEAR SIR:—The articles I am sending you to dispose of were gifts of dear friends, which only *urgent necessity* compels me to part with, and I am especially anxious that they shall not be sacrificed.

"The circumstances are peculiar, and painfully embarrassing; therefore I hope you will endeavor to realize as much as possible for them. Hoping to hear from you, I remain, very respectfully,

"Mrs. A. Lincoln."

"Sept. 25, 1867.

"W. H. Brady, Esq. :—My great, great sorrow and loss have made me painfully sensitive, but as my feelings and pecuniary comforts were never regarded or even recognized in the midst of my overwhelming bereavement—*now* that I am pressed in a most startling manner for means of subsistence, I do not know why I should shrink from an opportunity of improving my trying position.

"Being assured that all you do will be appropriately executed, and in a manner that will not startle me very greatly, and excite as little comment as possible, again I shall leave all in your hands.

" I am passing through a very painful ordeal, which the country, in remembrance of my noble and devoted husband, should have spared me.

" I remain, with great respect, very truly,

" MRS. LINCOLN.

" P. S.—As you mention that my goods have been valued at over $24,000, I will be willing to make a reduction of $8,000, and relinquish them for $16,000. If this is not accomplished, I will continue to sell and advertise largely until every article is sold.

" I must have means to live, at least in a medium comfortable state.

" M. L."

The letters are dated Chicago, and addressed to Mr. Brady, though every one of them was

written in New York; for when Mrs. L. left
the West for the East, she had settled upon no
definite plan of action.   Mr. Brady proposed
to show the letters to certain politicians, and ask
for money on a threat to publish them if his demands, as Mrs. Lincoln's agent, were not com
plied with.   When writing the letters I stood at
Mrs. Lincoln's elbow, and suggested that they
be couched in the mildest language possible.

"Never mind, Lizzie," she said; "anything to
raise the wind.   One might as well be killed for
a sheep as a lamb."

This latter expression was a favorite one of
hers; she meaning by it, that if one must be
punished for an act, such as theft for instance,
that the punishment would be no more severe if
a sheep were taken instead of a lamb.

Mr. Brady exhibited the letters quite freely,
but the parties to whom they were shown refused
to make any advances.   Meanwhile our stay at
the Union Place Hotel excited so much curiosity,

that a sudden movement was rendered expedient
to avoid discovery. We sent the large trunks
to 609 Broadway, packed the smaller ones, paid
our bills at the hotel, and one morning hastily
departed for the country, where we remained
three days. The movement was successful. The
keen-eyed reporters for the daily papers were
thrown off the scent, and when we returned to
the city we took rooms at the Brandreth House,
where Mrs. Lincoln registered as " Mrs. Morris."
I had desired her to go to the Metropolitan Hotel, and confide in the proprietors, as the Messrs.
Leland had always been very kind to her, treat-
ing her with distinguished courtesy whenever
she was their guest; but this she refused to do.

Several days passed, and Messrs. Brady and
Keyes were forced to acknowledge that their
scheme was a failure. The letters had been
shown to various parties, but every one declined
to act. Aside from a few dresses sold at small
prices to second-hand dealers, Mrs. Lincoln's

wardrobe was still in her possession. Her visit to New York had proved disastrous, and she was goaded into more desperate measures. Money she must have, and to obtain it she proposed to play a bolder game. She gave Mr. Brady permission to place her wardrobe on exhibition for sale, and authorized him to publish the letters in the *World*.

After coming to this determination, she packed her trunks to return to Chicago. I accompanied her to the depot, and told her good-by, on the very morning that the letters appeared in the *World*. Mrs. Lincoln wrote me the incidents of the journey, and the letter describes the story more graphically than I could hope to do. I suppress many passages, as they are of too confidential a nature to be given to the public:

" CHICAGO, October 6th.

" MY DEAR LIZZIE : —My ink is like myself and my spirits failing, so I write you to-day with a

pencil. I had a solitary ride to this place, as you
may imagine, varied by one or two amusing incidents. I found, after you left me, I could not continue in the car in which you left me, owing to
every seat's berth being engaged; so, being simple
Mrs. Clarke, I had to eat 'humble-pie' in a car
less commodious. My thoughts were too much
with my 'dry goods and interests' at 609 Broadway, to care much for my surroundings, as un-
comfortable as they were. In front of me sat
a middle-aged, gray-haired, respectable-looking
gentleman, who, for the whole morning, had the
page of the *World* before him which contained
my letters and business concerns. About four
hours before arriving at Chicago, a consequential-
looking man, of formidable size, seated himself
by him, and it appears they were entirely unknown to each other. The well-fed looking individual opened the conversation with the man
who had read the *World* so attentively, and the
conversation soon grew warm and earnest. The

war and its devastation engaged them. The bluffy individual, doubtless a Republican who had pocketed his many thousands, spoke of the widows of the land, made so by the war. My reading man remarked to him :

" ' Are you aware that Mrs. Lincoln is in indigent circumstances, and has to sell her clothing and jewelry to gain means to make life more endurable ? '

" The well-conditioned man replied : ' I do not blame her for selling her clothing, if she wishes it. I suppose *when sold* she will convert the proceeds into five-twenties to enable her to have means to be buried.'

" The *World* man turned towards him with a searching glance, and replied, with the haughtiest manner : ' That woman is not dead yet.'

" The discomfited individual looked down, never spoke another word, and in half an hour left his seat, and did not return.

" I give you word for word as the conversation

occurred. May it be found through the execution of my friends, Messrs Brady and Keyes, that 'that woman is not yet dead,' and being alive, she speaketh and gaineth valuable hearers. Such is life! Those who have been injured, how gladly the injurer would consign them to mother earth and forgetfulness! Hoping I should not be recognized at Fort Wayne, I thought I would get out at dinner for a cup of tea. * * * will show you what a creature of *fate* I am, as miserable as it sometimes is. I went into the dining-room alone, and was ushered up to the table, where, at its head, sat a very elegant-looking gentleman—at his side a middle-aged lady. My black veil was doubled over my face. I had taken my seat next to him—he at the head of the table, I at his left hand. I immediately *felt* a pair of eyes was gazing at me. I looked him full in the face, and the glance was earnestly returned. I sipped my water, and said: 'Mr. S., is this indeed you?' His face was as pale as the

table-cloth.   We entered into conversation, when
I asked him how long since he had left Chicago.
He replied, 'Two weeks since.'   He said, 'How
strange you should be on the train and I not
know it!'

"As soon as I could escape from the table, I did
so by saying, 'I must secure a cup of tea for a
lady friend with me who has a head-ache.'   I
had scarcely returned to the car, when he entered
it with a cup of tea borne by his own aristocratic
hands.   I was a good deal annoyed by seeing
him, and he was so agitated that he spilled half
of the cup over my *elegantly gloved* hands.   *He*
looked very sad, and I fancied 609 Broadway
occupied his thoughts.   I apologized for the absent lady who wished the cup, by saying that
'in my absence she had slipped out for it.'   His
heart was in his eyes, notwithstanding my veiled
face.   Pity for me, I fear, has something to do
with all this.   I never saw his manner *so* gentle
and sad.   This was nearly evening, and I did not

ot give up. How much
I miss you, tongue cannot tell. Forget my fright
and nervousness of the evening before. Of
course you were as innocent as a child in all you
did. I consider you my best living friend, and
I am struggling to be enabled some day to re-
pay you. Write me often, as you promised.

" Always truly yours,
" M. L."

It is not necessary for me to dwell upon the public history of Mrs. Lincoln's unfortunate venture. The question has been discussed in all the newspapers of the land, and these discussions are so recent that it would be useless to introduce them in these pages, even if I had an inclination to do so. The following, from the New York *Evening Express*, briefly tells the story:

" The attraction for ladies, and the curious and speculative of the other sex in this city, just now, is the grand exposition of Lincoln dresses at the office of Mr. Brady, on Broadway, a few doors south of Houston street. The publicity given to the articles on exhibition and for sale has excited the public curiosity, and hundreds of people, principally women with considerable leisure moments at disposal, daily throng the rooms of Mr. Brady, and give himself and his shop-woman more to do than either bargained for, when a lady, with face concealed with a veil, called and arranged for the sale of the superabundant clothing of a distinguished and titled, but nameless lady. Twenty-five dresses, folded or tossed about by frequent examinations, lie exposed upon a closed piano, and upon a lounge; shawls rich and rare are displayed upon the backs of chairs, but the more exacting obtain a better view and closer inspection by the lady attendant throwing them occasionally upon her shoulders, just to oblige, so that their appearance on promenade might be seen and admired. Furs, laces, and jewelry are in a glass case, but the 'four thousand dollars in gold' point outfit is kept in a paste-board box, and only shown on special request.

"The feeling of the majority of visitors is adverse to the course Mrs. Lincoln has thought proper to pursue, and the criticisms are as severe as the cavillings are persistent at the quality of some of the dresses. These latter are labelled at Mrs. Lincoln's own estimate, and prices range from $25 to $75—about 50 per cent. less than cost. Some of them, if not worn long, have been worn much; they are jagged under the arms and at the bottom of the skirt, stains are on the lining, and other objections present themselves to those who oscillate between the dresses and dollars, 'notwithstanding they have been worn by Madam Lincoln,' as a lady who looked from behind a pair of gold spectacles remarked. Other dresses, however, have scarcely been worn —one, perhaps, while Mrs. Lincoln sat for her picture, and from one the basting threads had not yet been removed. The general testimony is that the wearing apparel is high-priced, and some of the examiners say that the cost-figures must have been put on by the dress-makers; or, if such was not the case, that gold was 250 when they were purchased, and is now but 140—so that a dress for which $150 was paid at the rate of high figures cannot be called cheap at half that sum, after it has been worn considerable, and perhaps passed out of fashion. The peculiarity of the dresses is that the most of them are cut low-necked—a taste which some ladies attribute to Mrs. Lincoln's appreciation of her own bust.

" On Saturday last an offer was made for all the dresses. The figure named was less than the aggregate estimate placed on them. Mr. Brady, however, having no discretionary power, he declined to close the bargain, but notified Mrs. Lincoln by mail. Of course, as yet, no reply has been received. Mrs L. desires that the auction should be deferred till the 31st of the present month, and efforts made to dispose of the articles at private sale up to that time.

" A Mrs. C—— called on Mr. Brady this morning, and examined minutely each shawl. Before leaving the lady said that, at the time when there was a hesitancy about the President issuing the Emancipation Proclamation, she sent to Mrs. Lincoln an ashes-of-rose shawl, which was manufactured in China, forwarded to France, and thence to Mrs. C——, in New York. The

shawl, the lady remarked, was a very handsome
one, and should it come into the hands of Mr.
Brady to be sold, would like to be made aware
of the fact, so as to obtain possession again. Mr.
Brady promised to acquaint the ashes-of-rose
donor, if the prized article should be among
the two trunks of goods now on the way from
Chicago."

So many erroneous reports were circulated, that
I made a correct statement to one of the editors
of the New York *Evening News.* The article
based upon the memoranda furnished by me appeared in the *News* of Oct. 12, 1867. I reproduce a portion of it in this connection:

"Mrs. Lincoln feels sorely aggrieved at many of
the harsh criticisms that have been passed upon
her for travelling incognito. She claims that she
adopted this course from motives of delicacy,
desiring to avoid publicity. While here, she
spoke to but two former acquaintances, and these
two gentlemen whom she met on Broadway.

Hundreds passed her who had courted her good graces when she reigned supreme at the White House, but there was no recognition. It was not because she had changed much in personal appearance, but was merely owing to the heavy crape veil that hid her features from view.

"She seeks to defend her course while in this city—and with much force, too. Adverting to the fact that the Empress of France frequently disposes of her cast-off wardrobe, and publicly too, without being subjected to any unkind remarks regarding its propriety, she claims the same immunity here as is accorded in Paris to Eugenie. As regards her obscurity while in this city, she says that foreigners of note and position frequently come to our stores, and under assumed names travel from point to point throughout our vast domain, to avoid recognition and the inconveniences resulting from being known, though it even be in the form of honors. For herself she regards quiet preferable to ostentatious show, which would have cost her much indirectly, if not directly; and this she felt herself unable to bear, according to the measure of her present state of finances.

"In a recent letter to her bosom friend, Mrs. Elizabeth Keckley, Mrs. Lincoln pathetically remarks, 'Elizabeth, if evil come from this, pray for my deliverance, as I did it for the best.' This referred to her action in placing her personal effects before the public for sale, and to the harsh remarks that have been made thereon by some whom she had formerly regarded as her friends.

"As to the articles which belonged to Mr. Lincoln, they can all be accounted for in a manner satisfactory even to an over-critical public. During the time Mr. Lincoln was in office he was the recipient of several canes. After his death one was given to the Hon. Charles Sumner; another to Fred. Douglass; another to the Rev. H. H. Garnet of this city, and another to Mr. Wm. Slade, the present steward of the White House, who, in Mr. Lincoln's lifetime, was his messenger. This gentleman also received some of Mr. Lincoln's apparel, among which was his heavy gray shawl. Several other of the messengers employed about the White House came in for a share of the deceased President's effects.

"The shepherd plaid shawl which Mr. Lincoln wore during the milder weather, and which was rendered somewhat memorable as forming part of his famous disguise, together with the Scotch cap, when he wended his way secretly to the Capitol to be inaugurated as President, was given to Dr. Abbot, of Canada, who had been one of his warmest friends. During the war this gentleman, as a surgeon in the United States army, was in Washington in charge of a hospital, and thus became acquainted with the head of the nation.

" His watch, his penknife, his gold pencil, and his glasses are now in possession of his son Robert. Nearly all else than these few things have passed out of the family, as Mrs. Lincoln did not wish to retain them. But all were freely given away, and not an article was parted with for money.

" The Rev. Dr. Gurley of Washington was the spiritual adviser of the President and his family. They attended his church. When little ' Willie' died, he officiated at the funeral. He was a most intimate friend of the family, and when Mr. Lincoln lay upon his death-bed Mr. Gurley was by his side. He, as his clergyman, performed the funeral rites upon the body of the deceased President, when it lay cold in death at the City of Washington. He received the hat worn last by Mr. Lincoln, as we have before stated, and it is still retained by him.

" The dress that was worn by Mrs. Lincoln on the night of the assassination was presented to Mrs. Wm. Slade. It is a black silk with a little white stripe. Most of the other articles that adorned Mrs. Lincoln on that fatal night became the property of Mrs. Keckley. She has the most of them carefully stowed away, and intends keeping them during her life as mementos of a mournful event. The principal articles among these are the earrings, the bonnet, and the velvet cloak. The writer of this saw the latter on Thursday. It bears most palpable marks of the assassination, being completely bespattered with blood, that has dried upon its surface, and which can never be removed.

"A few words as regard the disposition and habits of Mrs. Lincoln. She is no longer the sprightly body she was when her very presence illumed the White House with gayety. Now she is sad and sedate, seeking seclusion, and maintaining communication merely with her most intimate personal friends. The most of her time she devotes to instructive reading within the walls of her boudoir. Laying her book aside spasmodically, she places her hand upon her forehead, as if ruminating upon something momentous. Then her hand wanders amid her heavy tresses, while she ponders for but a few seconds—then, by a sudden start, she approaches her writing-stand, seizes a pen, and indites a few hasty lines to some trusty friend, upon the troubles that weigh so heavily upon her. Speedily it is sent to the post-office; but, hardly has the mail departed from the city before she regrets her hasty letter, and would give much to recall it. But, too late, it is gone, and probably the secrets it contains are not confidentially kept by the party to whom it was addressed, and soon it furnishes inexhaustible material for gossip-loving people.

" As some citizens have expressed themselves desirous of aiding Mrs. Lincoln, a subscription-book was opened at the office of her agent, Mr. Brady, No. 609 Broadway, this morning. There is no limitation as to the amount which may be given, though there was a proposition that a dollar should be contributed by each person who came forward to inspect the goods. Had each person who handled these articles given this sum, a handsome amount would already have been realized.

" The colored people are moving in this matter. They intend to take up collections in their churches for the benefit of Mrs. Lincoln. They are enthusiastic, and a trifle from every African in this city would, in the aggregate, swell into an immense sum, which would be doubly acceptable to Mrs. Lincoln. It would satisfy her that the black people still have the memory of her deceased husband fresh in their minds.

" The goods still remain exposed to sale, but it is now announced that they will be sold at public auction on the 30th of this month, unless they be disposed of before that at private sale."

It is stated in the article that the " colored people are moving in this matter." The colored people were surprised to hear of Mrs. Lincoln's poverty, and the news of her distress called forth

14

strong sympathy from their warm, generous hearts. Rev. H. H. Garnet, of New York City, and Mr. Frederick Douglass, of Rochester, N. Y., proposed to lecture in behalf of the widow of the lamented President, and schemes were on foot to raise a large sum of money by contribution. The colored people recognized Abraham Lincoln as their great friend, and they were anxious to show their kind interest in the welfare of his family in some way more earnest and substantial than simple words. I wrote Mrs. Lincoln what we proposed to do, and she promptly replied, declining to receive aid from the colored people. I showed her letter to Mr. Garnet and Mr. Douglass, and the whole project was at once abandoned. She afterwards consented to receive contributions from my people, but as the services of Messrs. Douglass, Garnet, and others had been refused when first offered, they declined to take an active part in the scheme; so nothing was ever done. The following letters were written before Mrs.

Lincoln declined to receive aid from the colored people:

"183 BLEECKER ST., NEW YORK, October 16th, 1867.

"J. H. BRADY, ESQ. :—

"I have just received your favor, together with the circulars. I will do all that lies in my power, but I fear that will not be as much as you antici- pate. I think, however, that a contribution from the colored people of New York will be worth something in a moral point of view, and likely that will be the most that will be accomplished in the undertaking. I am thoroughly with you in the work, although but little may be done.

"I am truly yours,

"HENRY HIGHLAND GARNET.

"P. S.—I think it would be well if you would drop a line to Mr. Frederick Douglass, at Roches- ter, New York.

"H. H. G."

"ROCHESTER, Oct. 18, 1867.

"MY DEAR MRS. KECKLEY:—You judge me rightly—I am willing to do what I can to place the widow of our martyr President in the affluent position which her relation to that good man and to the country entitles her to. But I doubt the wisdom of getting up a series of lectures for that purpose; that is just the last thing that should be done. Still, if the thing is done, it should be done on a grand scale. The best speakers in the country should be secured for the purpose. You should not place me at the head nor at the foot of the list, but sandwich me between, for thus out of the way, it would not give *color* to the idea. I am to speak in Newark on Wednesday evening next, and will endeavor to see you on the subject. Of course, if it would not be too much to ask, I would gladly see Mrs. Lincoln, if this could be done in a quiet way without the reporters getting hold of it, and using it in some way to the prejudice of that already much abused lady. As I shall see you soon, there is less reason to write you at length.

> "I am, dear madam,
>> "With high respect,
>>> "Very truly yours,
>>>> "FREDERICK DOUGLASS."

"POTTSVILLE, Oct. 29, 1867.

"MY DEAR MRS. KECKLEY :—You know the drift of my views concerning the subscription for Mrs. Lincoln. Yet I wish to place them more distinctly before you, so that, if you have occasion to refer to me in connection with the matter, you can do so with accuracy and certainty.

"It is due Mrs. Lincoln that she should be indemnified, as far as money can do so, for the loss of her beloved husband. Honor, gratitude, and a manly sympathy, all say yes to this. I am willing to go farther than this, and say that Mrs. Lincoln herself should be the judge of the amount which shall be deemed sufficient, believing that she would not transcend reasonable limits. The obligation resting on the nation at large is great and increasing, but especially does it become colored men to recognize that obligation. It was the hand of Abraham Lincoln that broke the fetters of our enslaved people, and let them out of the house of bondage. When he was slain, our great benefactor fell, and left his wife and children to the care of those for whom he gave up all. Shame on the man or woman who, under such circumstances, would grudge a few paltry dollars, to smooth the pathway of such a widow! All this, and more, I feel and believe. But such is the condition of this question, owing to party feeling, and personal animosities now mixed up with it, that we are compelled to consider these in the effort we are making to obtain subscriptions.

" Now, about the meeting in Cooper Institute; I hold that that meeting should only be held in concert with other movements. It is bad generalship to put into the field only a fraction of your army when you have no means to prevent their being cut to pieces. It is gallant to go forth single-handed, but is it wise? I want to see something more than the spiteful *Herald* behind me when I step forward in this cause at the Cooper Institute. Let Mr. Brady out with his circulars, with his list of commanding names, let the *Herald* and *Tribune* give a united blast upon their bugles, let the city be placarded, and the doors of Cooper Institute be flung wide open, and the people, without regard to party, come up to the discharge of this national duty.

" Don't let the cause be made ridiculous by failure at the outset. Mr. Garnet and I could bear any mortification of this kind; but the cause could not. And our cause must not be damaged by any such generalship, which would place us in the van unsupported.

" I shall be at home by Saturday; please write me and let me know how matters are proceeding. Show this letter to Messrs. Brady and Garnet.

> "I am, dear madam,
>> "Very truly yours,
>>> "FREDERICK DOUGLASS."

> "ROCHESTER, Oct. 30, 1867.

"MY DEAR MRS. KECKLEY :—It is just possible that I may not take New York in my route homeward. In that case please write me directly at Rochester, and let me know fully how the subscription business is proceeding. The meeting here last night was a grand success. I speak again this evening, and perhaps at Reading tomorrow evening. My kind regards to all who think of me at 21, including Mrs. Lawrence.

> "Very truly yours,
>> "FREDK. DOUGLASS."

> "ROCHESTER, Nov. 10, 1867.

"MY DEAR MRS. KECKLEY :—I very easily read your handwriting. With practice you will not only write legibly but elegantly; so no more apologies for *bad* writing. Penmanship has always been one of my own deficiencies, and I know how to sympathize with you.

"I am just home, and find your letter awaiting me. You should have received an earlier answer but for this absence. I am sorry it will be impossible for me to see you before I go to Washington. I am leaving home this week for Ohio, and shall go from Ohio to Washington. I shall be in New York a day or two after my visit to Washington, and will see you there. Any public demonstration in which it will be desirable for me to take part, ought to come off the last of this month or the first of next. I thank you sincerely for the note containing a published letter of dear Mrs. Lincoln; both letters do credit to the excellent lady. I prize her beautiful letter to me very highly. It is the letter of a refined and spirited lady, let the world say what it will of her. I would write her a word of acknowledgment but

14*

for fear to burden her with correspondence. I am glad that Mr. Garnet and yourself saw Mr. Greeley, and that he takes the right view of the matter; but we want more than right views, and delay is death to the movement. What you now want is action and co-operation. If Mr. Brady does not for any reason find himself able to move the machinery, somebody else should be found to take his place; he made a good impression on me when I saw him, but I have not seen the promised simultaneous movement of which we spoke when together. This whole thing should be in the hands of some recognized solid man in New York. No man would be better than Mr. Greeley; no man in the State is more laughed at, and yet no man is more respected and trusted; a dollar placed in his hands would be as safe for the purpose as in a burglar-proof safe, and what is better still, everybody believes this. This testimonial must be more than a negro testimonial. It is a great national duty. Mr. Lincoln did everything for the black man, but he did it not for the black man's sake, but for the nation's sake. His life was given for the nation; but for being President, Mr. Lincoln would have been alive, and Mrs. Lincoln would have been a wife, and not a widow as now. Do all you can, dear Mrs. Keckley—nobody can do more than you in removing the mountains of prejudice towards that good lady, and opening the way of success in the plan.

"I am, dear madam, very truly yours,

"FREDERICK DOUGLASS."

Many persons called at 609 Broadway to examine Mrs. Lincoln's wardrobe, but as curiosity prompted each visit, but few articles were sold. Messrs. Brady & Keyes were not very energetic, and, as will be seen by the letters of Mrs. Lincoln, published in the Appendix, that lady ultimately lost all confidence in them. It was proposed to send circulars, stating Mrs. Lincoln's wants, and appealing to the generosity of the people for aid, broad-cast over the country; but the scheme failed. Messrs. Brady & Keyes were unable to obtain the names of prominent men, whom the people had confidence in, for the circular, to give character and responsibility to the movement—so the whole thing was abandoned. With the Rev. Mr. Garnet, I called on Mr. Greeley, at the office of the *Tribune*, in connection with this scheme. Mr. Greeley received us kindly, and listened patiently to our proposals—then said :

"I shall take pleasure in rendering you what assistance I can, but the movement must be engineered by responsible parties. Messrs. Brady & Keyes are not the men to be at the head of it. Nobody knows who they are, or what they are. Place the matter in the hands of those that the people know and have some confidence in, and then there will be a chance for success."

We thanked Mr. Greeley for his advice, for we

believed it to be good advice, and bowed ourselves out of his room. When Messrs. Brady &
Keyes were informed of the result of our interview, they became very much excited, and denounced Mr. Greeley as "an old fool." This put
an end to the circular movement. The enterprise
was nipped in the bud, and with the bud withered Mrs. Lincoln's last hope for success. A portion of the wardrobe was then taken to Providence, to be exhibited, but without her consent.
Mr. Brady remarked that the exhibition would
bring in money, and as money must be raised,
this was the last resort. He was of the impression that Mrs. Lincoln would approve of any
movement, so it ended in success. This, at least,
is a charitable view to take of the subject. Had
the exhibition succeeded in Providence, it is my
opinion that the agents of Brady & Keyes would
now be travelling over the country, exposing Mrs.
Lincoln's wardrobe to the view of the curious, at
so much per head. As is well known, the city

authorities refused to allow the exhibition to take place in Providence ; therefore Mr. Brady returned to New York with the goods, and the travelling show scheme, like the circular scheme, was abandoned. Weeks lengthened into months, and at Mrs. Lincoln's urgent request I remained in New York, to look after her interests. When she left the city I engaged quiet lodgings in a private family, where I remained about two months, when I moved to 14 Carroll Place, and became one of the regular boarders of the house. Mrs. Lincoln's venture proved so disastrous that she was unable to reward me for my services, and I was compelled to take in sewing to pay for my daily bread. My New York expedition has made me richer in experience, but poorer in purse. During the entire winter I have worked early and late, and practised the closest economy. Mrs. Lincoln's business demanded much of my time, and it was a constant source of trouble to me. When Mrs. L. left for the West, I expected to be able to return to Washington in one week from the day; but unforeseen difficulties arose, and I have been detained in the city for several months. As I am writing the concluding pages of this book, I have succeeded in closing up Mrs. Lincoln's imprudent business arrangement at 609 Broadway. The firm of Brady & Keyes is dissolved, and Mr. Keyes has adjusted the account. The story is told in a few words. On the 4th of March I received the following invoice from Mr. Keyes :

"March 4, '68.

"*Invoice of articles sent to Mrs. A. Lincoln:*
    1 Trunk.
    1 Lace dress.
    1 do. do. flounced.
    5 Lace shawls.
    3 Camel hair shawls.
    1 Lace parasol cover.
    1 do. handkerchief.

1 Sable boa.

1 White do.

1 Set furs.

2 Paisley shawls.

2 Gold bracelets.

16 Dresses.

2 Opera cloaks.

1 Purple shawl.

1 Feather cape.

28 yds. silk.

ARTICLES SOLD.

1 Diamond ring.

3 Small   do.

1 Set furs.

1 Camel hair shawl.

1 Red   do.

2 Dresses.

1 Child's shawl.

1 Lace Chantilly shawl."

The charges of the firm amounted to eight hundred dollars. Mrs. Lincoln sent me a check for this amount. I handed this check to Mr. Keyes, and he gave me the following receipt:

"Received, New York, March 4, 1868, of Mrs. Abraham Lincoln, eight hundred and twenty dollars by draft on American National Bank, New York.

"S. C. Keyes."

I packed the articles invoiced, and expressed the trunks to Mrs. Lincoln at Chicago. I then demanded and received a receipt worded as follows:

"Received, New York, March 4, 1868, of Mrs. Abraham Lincoln, eight hundred and twenty dollars in full of all demands of every kind up to date.

"S. C. Keyes."

This closed up the business, and with it I close the imperfect story of my somewhat romantic life. I have experienced many ups and

downs, but still am stout of heart. The labor of
a lifetime has brought me nothing in a pecuniary way. I have worked hard, but fortune,
fickle dame, has not smiled upon me. If poverty
did not weigh me down as it does, I would not
now be toiling by day with my needle, and
writing by night, in the plain little room on the
fourth floor of No. 14 Carroll Place. And yet I
have learned to love the garret-like room. Here,
with Mrs. Amelia Lancaster as my only companion, I have spent many pleasant hours, as
well as sad ones, and every chair looks like an old
friend. In memory I have travelled through the
shadows and the sunshine of the past, and the
bare walls are associated with the visions that
have come to me from the long-ago. As I love
the children of memory, so I love every article in
this room, for each has become a part of memory
itself. Though poor in worldly goods, I am rich
in friendships, and friends are a recompense for
·all the woes of the darkest pages of life. For

sweet friendship's sake, I can bear more burdens than I have borne.

The letters appended from Mrs. Lincoln to myself throw a flood of light upon the history of the " old clothes " speculation in New York.

APPENDIX.

LETTERS FROM MRS. LINCOLN TO MRS. KECKLEY.

"CHICAGO, Sunday Morning, Oct. 6.

"MY DEAR LIZZIE:—I am writing this morning with a broken heart after a sleepless night of great mental suffering. R. came up last evening like a maniac, and almost threatening his life, looking iike death, because the letters of the *World* were published in yesterday's paper. I could not refrain from weeping when I saw him so miserable. But yet, my dear good Lizzie, was it not to protect myself and help others—and was not my motive and action of the purest kind?

Pray for me that this cup of affliction may pass from me, or be sanctified to me. I weep whilst I am writing. * * * * I pray for death this morning. Only my darling Taddie prevents my taking my life. I shall have to endure a round of newspaper abuse from the Republicans because I dared venture to relieve a few of my wants. Tell Mr. Brady and Keyes not to have a line of mine ·once more in print I am nearly losing my reason.

" Your friend,

" M. L."

" Chicago, Oct. 8.

" My dear Lizzie :—Bowed down with suffering and anguish, again I write you. As we might have expected, the Republicans are falsifying me, and doing *just* as they did when they prevented the Congressional appropriation. Mrs. —— knows something about these same people. As her husband *is living* they dare not utter all they would desire to speak. You know yourself how innocently I have acted, and from the best and purest motives. They will *howl on* to prevent my disposing of my things. What a *vile, vile* set they are! The *Tribune* here, Mr. White's paper, wrote a very beautiful editorial yesterday in my behalf; yet knowing that I have been deprived of my rights by the party, I suppose I would be *mobbed* if I ventured out. What a world of anguish this is—and how I have been made to suffer! *   *   * You would not recognize me now. The glass shows me a pale, wretched, haggard face, and my dresses are like bags on me. And all because I was doing what I felt to be my duty. Our minister, Mr. Swazey, called on me yesterday and said I had done perfectly right. Mrs. F—— says every one speaks in the same way. The politicians, knowing they have deprived me of my just rights, would prefer to see me starve, rather than dispose of my things. They will prevent the sale of anything, so I have telegraphed for them. I hope you have received from B. the letters I have consigned to his care. See to this. Show none of them. Write me every day.

"M. L."

"CHICAGO, Wednesday, October 9th.

"MY DEAR LIZZIE:—It appears as if the fiends had let loose, for the Republican papers are tearing me to pieces in this border ruffian West. If I had committed murder in every city in this *blessed Union*, I could not be more traduced. And you know how innocent I have been of the intention of doing wrong. A piece in the morning *Tribune*, signed ' B,' pretending to be a lady, says there is no doubt Mrs. L.— *is* deranged—has been for years past, and will end her life in a lunatic asylum. They would doubtless like me to begin it *now*. Mr. S., a very kind, sympathizing minister, has been with me this morning, and has now gone to see Mr. Medill, of the *Tribune*, to know if *he* sanctioned his paper publishing such an article.   *   *   * Pray for me, dear Lizzie, for I am very miserable and broken-hearted. Since writing this, I have just received a letter from Mr. Keyes, begging and pleading with me to allow them to use my name for donations. I think I will consent.   *   *

"Truly yours,

M. L."

" CHICAGO, Sunday, Oct. 13.

" MY DEAR LIZZIE:—I am greatly disappointed, having only received one letter from you since we parted, which was dated the day after. Day after day I sent to Mrs. F. for letters. After your promise of writing to me every other day, I can scarcely understand it. I hope to-morrow will bring me a letter from you. How much I miss you cannot be expressed. I hope you have arrived safely in Washington, and will tell me everything.   *   *   * Was there ever such

cruel newspaper abuse lavished upon an un-
offending woman as has been showered upon my
devoted head? The people of this ungrateful
country are like the 'dogs in the manger;'
will neither do anything themselves, nor allow me
to improve my own condition. What a Government we have! All their abuse lavished upon
me only lowers themselves in the estimation of
all true-hearted people. The Springfield *Journal*
had an editorial a few days since, with the
important information that Mrs. Lincoln had
been known to be *deranged* for years, and
should be *pitied* for all her *strange acts.* I
should have been *all right* if I had allowed *them*
to take possession of the White House. In the
comfortable stealings by contracts from the Government, these low creatures are allowed to hurl
their malicious wrath at me, with no one to
defend me or protect me, if I should starve.
These people injure themselves far more than
they could do me, by their lies and villany.
Their aim is to prevent my goods being sold, or

anything being done for me. *In this*, I very much fear, they have succeeded.

" Write me, my dear friend, your candid opinion about everything. I wished to be made better off, quite as much to improve your condition as well as for myself.   *   *   *   Two weeks ago, dear Lizzie, we were in that *den* of discomfort and dirt. *Now* we are far asunder. Every other day, for the past week, I have had a chill, brought on by excitement and suffering of mind. In the midst of it I have moved into my winter quarters, and am now very comfortably situated. My parlor and bedroom are very sweetly furnished. I am lodged in a handsome house, a very kind, good, *quiet* family, and their meals are excellent. I consider myself fortunate in all this. I feel assured that the Republicans, who, to cover up their own perfidy and neglect, have used every villanous falsehood in their power to injure me— I fear they have *more* than succeeded, but if their day of reckoning does not come in this world, it *will surely* in the next.   *   *   *   *

" *Saturday.*—I have determined to shed no more tears over all their cruel falsehoods, yet, just now, I feel almost forsaken by God and man—except by the *latter* to be vilified. Write me all that Keyes and Brady think of the result. For myself, after *such* abuse, I *expect* nothing. Oh ! that I could see you. Write me, dear Lizzie, if only a line ; I cannot understand your silence. Hereafter direct your letters to Mrs. A. Lincoln, 460 West Washington street, Chicago, Ill., care of D. Cole. Remember 460. I am always so anxious to hear from you, I am feeling so *friendless* in the world. I remain always your affectionate friend.　　　　　　　　　　　M. L."

POSTSCRIPT TO LETTER OF OCT. 24.

" I cannot send this letter off without writing you two little incidents that have occurred within the past week. We may call it *justice* rendered for *evil words*, to say the least. There is a paper published in Chicago called the *Republican*,

owned and published by Springfield men. Each
morning since my return it has been thrown at
my door, filled with abuse of myself. Four days
ago a piece appeared in it, asking 'What right
had Mrs. L. to diamonds and laces?' Yesterday
morning an article appeared in the same paper,
announcing that the day previous, at the house of
Mr. Bunn (the owner of the paper), in Springfield, Illinois—the house had been entered at 11
in the morning, by burglars, and had been robbed
of *five* diamond rings, and a quantity of fine laces.
This morning's paper announces the recovery of
these articles. Mr. Bunn, who made his hundreds
of thousands off our government, is running this
paper, and denouncing the wife of the man from
whom he obtained his means. I enclose you the
article about the recovery of the goods. A few
years ago he had a *small grocery* in S———.
These facts can be authenticated. Another case
in point : The evening I left my house to come
here, the young daughter of one of my neighbors

in the same block, was in a house not a square off, and in a childish manner was regretting that I could not retain my house. The man in the house said: 'Why waste your tears and regrets on Mrs. Lincoln?' An hour afterward the husband and wife went out to make a call, doubtless to gossip about me; on their return they found their young boy had almost blinded himself with gunpowder. Who will say that the cry of the 'widow and fatherless' is disregarded in *His* sight! If man is not merciful, God will be in his own time. M. L."

"CHICAGO, October 29.

"MY DEAR LIZZIE:—I received a very pleasant note from Mr. F. Douglass on yesterday. I will reply to it this morning, and enclose it to you to hand or send him immediately. In this morning's *Tribune* there was a little article *evidently* designed to make capital *against* me just now—that *three* of my brothers were in the Southern army during the war. If they had been friendly with me they might have said they were *half* brothers of Mrs. L., whom she had not known since they were infants; and as she left Kentucky at an early age her sympathies were entirely Republican—that her feelings were entirely with the North during the war, and always. I never failed to urge my husband to be an *extreme* Republican, and now, in the day of my trouble, you see how *this* very party is trying to work against me. Tell Mr. Douglass, and every one, how deeply my feelings were enlisted in the cause of freedom. Why *harp* upon these *half* brothers, whom I never knew since they were infants, and scarcely then, for my early home was truly at a *boarding* school. Write to him all this, and talk it to every one else. If we succeed I will soon send you enough for a very large supply of trimming material for the winter. Truly,

"M. L."

" MY DEAR LIZZIE :—Your letter of last Wednesday is received, and I cannot refrain from expressing my surprise that before now K. and B. did not go out in *search* of names, and have sent forth all those circulars. Their conduct is becoming mysterious. We have heard enough of *their talk*—it is time now they should be *acting*. Their delay, I fear, has ruined the business. The circulars should all have been out before the *election*. I cannot understand their slowness. As Mr. Greeley's home is in New York, he could certainly have been found had he *been sought ;* and there are plenty of other good men in New York, as well as himself. I venture to say, that *before* the election not a circular will be sent out. I begin to think they are making a political business of *my clothes*, and not for *my* benefit either. Their delay in acting is becoming very suspicious. Their slow, bad management is *ruining* every prospect of success. I fear you are only losing your time in New York, and that I shall be left *in debt* for what I am owing the firm. I have written to K. and B., and they do nothing that I request. I want neither Mr. Douglass nor Garnet to lecture in my behalf. The conduct in New York is disgusting me with the whole business. I cannot understand what they have been about. Their delay has only given the enemies time to *gather* strength; what does it all mean? Of course give the lady at 609 permission to sell the dresses cheaper. * * * I am feeling wretchedly over the slowness and *do-nothing* style of B. & K. I believe in my heart I am being used as a tool for party purposes; and they do not design sending out a circular. * * *

"Your friend,   M. L."

"Chicago, Nov. 9, 1867.

"My dear Lizzie:—* * * Did you receive a letter a few days since, with one enclosed for F. Douglass? also a printed letter of mine, which I wished him to read? Do write me every other day at least, I am so *nervous and miserable.* And Lizzie, dear, I fear we have not the *least* chance of success. *Do* remain in New York a little longer, and occupy yourself with the sewing of your friends. *Then* I shall be able to learn *some*thing about my business. In *your heart* you know there will be no success. *Why* do you not candidly express yourself to me? Write me, if only a few lines, and that very frequently. R. called up on yesterday, with Judge Davis. * * * R. goes with Judge D. on Tuesday, to settle the estate, which will give us each about $25,000, with the income I told you of, $1,700 a year for each of us. You made a mistake about my house costing $2,700—it was $1,700. The $22,000 Congress gave me I spent for house and furniture, which, owing to the smallness of my income, I was obliged to leave. I mention about the division of the estate to you, dear Lizzie, because when it is done the *papers* will harp upon

15*

it. You can explain everything in New York; please do so to every one. Please see H. G., if it should come out in the papers. I had hoped, if something was gained, to have immediately placed *you* in more pleasant circumstances. Do urge F. D. to add his name to the circular; also get them to have Beecher's. There must not be an hour's delay in this. R. is very spiteful at present, and I think hurries up the division to *cross* my purposes. He mentioned yesterday that he was going to the Rocky Mountains so soon as Edgar Welles joined him. He is very *deep.* * * * Write me, *do*, when you receive this. Your silence pains me.

> " Truly yours,
>
> " M. L."

" CHICAGO, Nov. 9.

" MY DEAR LIZZIE:—I closed and sent off my letter before I had finished all I had to say. Do not hint to K. or B., or any one else, my doubts of

them, *only watch them.* As to S., so many falsehoods are told in the papers that all the stuff
about his wife and himself may be untrue. I
hope it may prove so. I received a letter from
Keyes this morning. I believe I wrote you that
I had. How hard it is that I cannot see and
talk with you in this time of great, *great* trouble.
I feel as if I had not a friend in the world save
yourself. *   * I sometimes wish myself out
of this world of sorrow and care. I fear my fine
articles at B.'s are getting pulled to pieces and
soiled. I do not wish you to leave N. Y. without having the finest articles packed up and returned to me. The *single* white camel's hair
shawl and the two Paisleys I wish returned to
me, if none of them are sold. Do you think
there is the least chance of *their* being sold? I
will give you a list of the articles I wish
returned to me from Mr. Brady's before *you
leave* New York for Washington.

"1 Camel's hair shawl, double black centre.

1 Camel's hair shawl, double white centre.

1 Single white camel's hair shawl.

2 Paisley shawls—white.

1 Pair bracelets and diamond ring.

1 Fine lace handkerchief.

3 Black lace shawls.

2 Black lama shawls.

1 Dress, silk unmade, white and black.

1 White boa.

1 Russian sable boa.

1 Russian sable cape.

1 A. sable cape, cuffs and muff.

1 Chinchilla set.

"The lace dress, flounce, and shawl, if there is no possibility of their being sold. Also all other fine articles return me, save the dresses which, with prices lowered, *may be sold.* *   *

"M. L."

"CHICAGO, Nov. 15, '67.

"MY DEAR KECKLEY:—Your last letter has been

received, and believe me, I duly appreciate your great interest in my affairs. I hope the day *may* arrive when I can return your kindness in *more* than words. As you are aware of my beloved husband's great indulgence to me in pecuniary matters, thereby allowing me to indulge in bestowing favors on those whom I considered worthy of it, it is in this respect I feel chiefly the humiliation of my small circumscribed income. If Congress, or the Nation, had given me the four years' salary, I should have been able to live as the widow of the great President Lincoln should, with sufficient means to give liberally to all benevolent objects, and at my death should have left at least half of it to the freedmen, for the liberty of whom his precious sacred life was sacrificed. The men who prevented *this* being done by their villanous unscrupulous falsehoods, are no friends of the colored race, and, as you well know, have led Johnson on in his wicked course.

" ' *God is just,*' and the day of retribution will

come to all such, if not in this world, in the great
hereafter, to which those hoary-headed sinners are
so rapidly hastening, with an innocent conscience.
I did not feel it necessary to raise my weak
woman's voice against the persecutions that have
assailed me emanating from the tongues of such
men as Weed & Co. I have felt that their infamous false lives was a sufficient vindication of my
character. They have never forgiven me for
standing between my pure and noble husband and
themselves, when, for their own vile purposes,
they would have led him into error. *All this*
the country knows, and why should I dwell
longer on it? In the blissful home where my
worshipped husband dwells God is ever merciful,
and it is the consolation of my broken heart that
my darling husband is ever retaining the devoted
love which he always so abundantly manifested
for his wife and children in this life. I feel
assured his watchful, loving eyes are always watch-
ing over us, and he is fully aware of the wrong

and injustice permitted his family by a country he lost his life in protecting. I write earnestly, because I feel very deeply. It appears to me a very remarkable coincidence, that most of the good feeling regarding my straitened circumstances proceeds from the colored people, in whose cause my noble husband was so largely interested. Whether we are successful or not, Mr. F. Douglass and Mr. Garnet will always have my most grateful thanks. They are very noble men. If any *favorable* results should crown their efforts, you may well believe at my death, whatever sum it may be, will be bequeathed to the colored people, who are very near my heart. In yesterday's paper it was announced that Gov. Andrew's family were having $100,000 contributed to them. Gov. A. was a good man, but what did *he* do compared to President Lincoln? Right and left the latter gave, when he had but little to bestow, and in consequence his family are now feeling it; yet for my life I would not recall a dollar he ever gave. Yet his favorite expression, when I have playfully alluded to the 'rainy day' that might be in store for *himself and his own* on several occasions, he has looked at me so earnestly and replied, 'Cast your bread upon the waters.' Although the petty sum of $22,000 was an insufficient return for Congress to make me, and allowanced to its meagreness by men who traduced and vilified the loved wife of the great man who *made them*, and from whom they amassed great fortunes—for *Weed, and Seward, and R.* did this last. And yet, *all this* was permitted by an American people, who owed *their* remaining a nation to my husband! I have dwelt too long on this painful subject, but when I have been compelled from a pitiful income to make a boarding-house of my home, as I now am doing, think you that it does not rankle in my heart?

"Fortunately, with my husband's great, great love for me—the knowledge of this future for his

petted and idolized wife was spared him, and yet
I feel in my heart *he* knows it all. Mr. Sumner,
the intimate friend of better days, called to see
me two or three weeks since—he who had been
an habitué of the White House—both the rooms
of the President and my own reception-room, in
either place he was always sure of a heartfelt welcome; my present situation must have struck a
painful chord in his noble, sympathizing heart.
And yet, when I endeavored to ameliorate my condition, the cry has been so fearful against me as to
cause me to forget my own identity, and suppose
I had plundered the nation, indeed, and committed murder. This, certainly, cannot be America,
'the land of the *free*,' the 'home of the *brave*.'
The evening before Mr. Sumner's last call I had
received Mr. Douglass's letter; I mentioned the
circumstance to Mr. Sumner, who replied: 'Mr.
Frederick Douglass is a very noble, talented man,
and I know of no one who writes a more beautiful letter.' I am sending you a long letter,

Lizzie, but I rely a great deal on your indulgence. My fear is that you will not be able to decipher the scrawl written *so* hastily.

> " I remain, truly yours,
> " MARY LINCOLN."

> " CHICAGO, Nov. 17.

" MY DEAR LIZZIE :—By the time you receive this note, you will doubtless find the papers *raving* over the large income which we are each *said* to have. Knowing exactly the amount we each will have, which I have already informed you, I was going to say, I have been shocked at the *fabulous* sum set down to each, but I have learned not to be surprised at anything. Of course it is gotten up to defeat success. *You* will *now* see the necessity for those circulars being issued weeks since. I enclose you a scrap from yesterday's *Times* of C., marked No. 1; also No. 2, to-day's *Times*. The sum of $11,000 has been subtracted in twenty-four hours from the same paper. If it continues for a few days longer, it will soon be right. It is a secesh paper—says Congress gave me $25,000 as a *present*, besides $20,000 of remaining salary. The $25,000 *you* know to be utterly false. You can show this note to B. & K., also the scraps sent. Let no one see them but themselves, and then burn them. It is all just as I expected—that when the division took place, a 'mountain would be made of a mole-hill.' And I fear it will succeed in injuring the premeditated plans. If the *war rages*, the *Evening News* might simply say that the sum assigned each was false; that $75,000 was the sum the administrator, Judge Davis, filed his bonds for. But by all means *my authority* must not be given. And then the *Evening News* can descant on the $25,000 each, with income of $1,700 each, and Mrs. Lincoln's share, she not being able to touch any of her sons' portion. My *word* or *testimony* must not appear in the article; only the paper must speak *decidedly.* It must be managed very judiciously, and without a day's delay.

"Yours truly,

"M. L."

"Nov 17—(Private for yourself).

"LIZZIE:—Show the note enclosed with this to B. & K.; do not let them retain it an instant after reading, nor the printed articles. I knew these falsehoods would be circulated when the estate was divided. What *has* been the cause of the delay about the circulars? I fear, between ourselves, we have reason to distrust those men, ——. Whatever is raised by the colored people, I solemnly give my word, at my death it shall *all*, every cent, be returned to them. And out of the sum, if it is $50,000, *you* shall have $5,000 at my death; and I cannot live long, suffering as I am now doing. If $25,000 is raised by your people, you shall have the sum at my death; and in either event, the

$25,000 raised, or $50,000, I will give you $300 a year, and the promised sum at my death. It will make your life easier. I have more faith in F. D.'s and G.'s efforts, than in B. & K., I assure you. This division has been trumped up just now through spite. * * I have written to Judge Davis for an exact statement, which I will send to you when received. Write if any thing is doing. * * *

"Truly,

"M. L."

"CHICAGO, November 21.

"MY DEAR LIZZIE:—Your letter of Tuesday is just received. I have just written B. a note of thanks for his kindness; also requesting the articles of which I gave you a list. Do see Keyes about it; K. will have it done. And will you *see* that they are forwarded to *me* before *you* leave New York? K. sent me a telegram on yesterday that eight names were on the circulars, and that they would be sent out *immediately*. What success do you think they will have? By all means assure K. & B. I have great confidence in them. These circulars must bring some money. Your letter made me quite sad. Talk to K. & B. of the *grateful feelings* I express towards them. Do pet up B., and see my things returned to me. Can you not, dear Lizzie, be employed in sewing for some of your lady friends in New York until December 1st? If I *ever* get any money you will be well remembered, be assured. R. and a party of young men leave for the Rocky Mountains next Monday, to be absent three weeks. If the circulars are sent out, of course the *blasts* will be blown over again. So R. is out of the way *at the time*, and money comes in, I will not care. Write the hour you receive this. I hope they will send out 150,000 circulars. Urge K. & B. to do this.

"Your friend,

"M. L."

"Saturday Morning, November 23d.

"MY DEAR LIZZIE :—Although I am suffering with a fearful headache to-day, yet, as your note of Wednesday is received, I must write. I am grieved to find that you are so wretchedly low-spirited. * * * On Wednesday, the 20th of November, K. sent me the telegram I send you. If he is not in earnest, what does it mean ? What is the rate of expenses that B. has gone to in my business, that he dares to withhold my immense amount of goods? Do you believe they *intend* sending out those circulars? Of course you will be well rewarded if we have any success, but as to $500 'now,' I have it not for myself, or any one else. Pray, what does B. propose to charge for *his expenses?* I pray God there will be some success, although, dear Lizzie, entirely between ourselves, I fear I am in villanous hands. As to money, I haven't it for myself just now, even if nothing comes in. When I get my things back, if ever, from ——, I will send you some of those dresses to dispose of at Washington for your own benefit. If we get something, *you* will find that *promises* and performance for *this* life will be forthcoming.   *   *   *   *   It is *mysterious* why B. NEVER writes, and K. *once*, perhaps, in three weeks. All this is very strange.   *   *

                                        " M. L."

                              "CHICAGO, Sunday, Nov. 24th.

"MY DEAR LIZZIE :—I wrote you on yesterday and am aware it was not a pleasant letter, although I wrote what I fear will turn out to be *truths*. It will be two weeks to-morrow since the legally attested consent from me was received by B. and K., and yet *names* have not been obtained for it, when last heard from.   *   *
However, we will soon see for ourselves. If you and I are honest in our motives and intentions, it is no reason *all* the world is so.   *   *   *
If I should gain nothing pecuniarily by the loud cry that has been made over my affairs, it has

been a losing game indeed. *   *   *   *
And the laugh of the world will be against
me if it turns out as I *now* think; there is
no doubt it will be *all* failure. If they had
issued those circulars when they should have
done, before the election, then it would have
been all right. Alas! alas! what a mistake it
has all been! I have thought seriously over the
whole business, and know what I am about. I
am grateful for the sympathy of Mr. F. Douglass
and Mr. Garnet. I see that F. D. is advertised
to lecture in Chicago some time this winter. Tell
him, for me, he must call and see me; give him
my number. If I had been able to retain a
house, I should have offered him apartments
when he came to C.; as it is, I have to content
myself with lodgings. An ungrateful country
this! I very much fear the malignity of Seward,
Weed, and R. will operate in Congress the coming
winter, and that I will be denounced *there*, with
their infamous and villanous falsehoods. The

father of wickedness and lies will get those men when they 'pass away;' and such fiends as they are, always linger in this mortal sphere. The agitation of mind has very much impaired my health. * * * * Why, why was not *I* taken when my darling husband was called from my side? I have been allowed no rest by those who, in my desolation, should have protected me. * * * * How dearly I should love to see you *this very sad day.* Never, dear Lizzie, think of my great nervousness the night before we parted; I had been so harassed with my fears. * * * *

"Always yours,

"M. L."

"December 26.

"My dear Lizzie :—Your letters just received. I have just written to K. to withdraw the C. Go to him yourself the moment you receive this. The idea of Congress doing anything is ridiculous. How much —— could effect *if he chose*, through others. Go to B. & K. the moment you receive this.

" Yours, M. L."

" CHICAGO, December 27.

" DEAR LIZZIE :—I wrote you a few lines on yesterday. I have twice written to Mr. K. to have the C. stopped. Go and see him on the subject. I believe any more newspaper attacks would *lay me low* * * * As *influence* has passed away from me with my husband, my slightest act is misinterpreted. ' *Time makes all things* right.' I am positively suffering for a decent dress. I see Mr. A. and *some recent* visitors eyeing my clothing askance. * * Do send my black merino dress to me very soon ; I must dress better in the future. I tremble at the bill that B. & K. may send me, I am so illy prepared to meet any expense. All my articles not sold must be sent to me. I leave *this* place

early in the spring; had you better not go with me and share my fortunes, for a year or more?
*   *   *Write.*

"Yours, etc.,   M. L."

"CLIFTON HOUSE, January 12.

" MY DEAR LIZZIE:—Your last letter was received a day or two since. I have moved my quarters to *this house*, so please direct all your letters *here*. Why did *you* not urge them *not* to take my goods to Providence? For heaven's sake see K. & B. when you receive this, and have them immediately returned to me, *with their bill.* I am so miserable I feel like taking my own life. My darling boy, my Taddie *alone*, I *fully* believe, prevents the deed. Your letter announcing that my clothes* were to be paraded in Europe—those

---

* The clothes that I have given for the benefit of Wilberforce College. They have been deeded to Bishop Payne, who will do with them as he thinks best, for the cause to which they are dedicated. The letter on page 366 will explain more fully.

I gave you—has almost turned me wild. R. would go *raving distracted* if such a thing was done. If you have the *least regard* for *our reason*, pray write to the bishop that it *must* not be done. How little did I suppose you would do *such a thing;* you cannot imagine how much my overwhelming sorrows would be increased. May kind Heaven turn your heart, and have you write that *this* exhibition must not be attempted. R. would blast us all if you were to have this project carried out. Do remember *us* in our unmitigated anguish, and have those clothes, worn on those fearful occasions, recalled. * * I am positively dying with a broken heart, and the probability is that I shall be living but a *very* short time. May we all meet in a better world, where *such grief* is unknown. Write me all about yourself. I should like you to have about four black widow's caps, just such as I had made in the fall in New York, sent to me. * * * Of course you would not suppose, if I had you come out here and work for me six weeks, I would not pay your expenses and pay you as you made *each* dress. The probability is that I shall need *few* more clothes ; my rest, I am inclined to believe, is *near at hand.* Go to B. & K., and have my clothes sent me without further publicity. * * * I am feeling too weak to write more to-day. Why are you so silent? For the sake of *humanity*, if not *me* and my children, *do not* have those black clothes displayed in Europe. The thought has almost whitened every hair of my head. Write when you receive this.

" Your friend,   M. L."

"New York City, Jan. 1st, 1868.

" Bishop Payne, D.D.—Dear Sir:—Allow me to donate certain valuable relics, to be exhibited for the benefit of Wilberforce University, where my son was educated, and whose life was sacrificed for liberty. These sacred relics were presented

to me by Mrs. Lincoln, after the assassination of
our beloved President. Learning that you were
struggling to get means to complete the college
that was burned on the day our great emancipa-
tor was assassinated, prompted me to donate, in
trust to J. P. Ball (agent for Wilberforce College), the identical cloak and bonnet worn by
Mrs. Lincoln on that eventful night. On the
cloak can be seen the life-blood of Abraham Lincoln. This cloak could not be purchased from
me, though many have been the offers for it. I
deemed it too *sacred* to sell, but donate it for
the cause of educating the four millions of slaves
liberated by our President, whose private character
I revere. You well know that I had every chance
to learn the true man, being constantly in the
White House during his whole administration.
I also donate the glove* worn on his precious
hand at the last inaugural reception. This glove

* I have since concluded to retain the glove as a precious
souvenir of our beloved President.

bears the marks of thousands who shook his hand on that last and great occasion. This, and many other relics, I hope you will receive in the name of the Lincoln fund. I also donate the dress worn by Mrs. Lincoln at the last inaugural address of President Lincoln. Please recéive these from—   Your sister in Christ,

"L. Keckley."

"Clifton House, Jan. 15, 1868.

"My dear Lizzie:—You will think I am sending you a deluge of letters. I am so very sad to-day, that I feel that I must write you. I went out last evening with Tad, on a little business, in a street car, heavily veiled, very imprudently having *my month's living* in my pocket-book— and, on return, found it gone. The loss I deserve for being so careless, but it comes very hard on poor me. Troubles and misfortunes·are fast overwhelming me; may *the end* soon come. I lost $82, and quite a new pocket-book. I am very, very anxious about that bill B. & K. may bring in. Do go, dear Lizzie, and implore them to be moderate, for I am in a very narrow place. Tell them, I pray you, of this last loss. As they have not been successful (BETWEEN OURSELVES), and only given me great sorrow and trouble, I think their demand should be very small. (Do not mention this to them.) *Do*, dear Lizzie, go to 609, and talk to them on this subject. Let my things be sent to me immediately, and *do* see to it, that nothing is left behind. I can afford to lose nothing they have had placed in their hands. I am literally suffering for my black dress. Will you send it to me when you receive this? I am looking very shabby. I hope you have entirely recovered. *Write* when you receive this.

"Very truly yours,　　　M. L."

"CHICAGO, Feb. 7.

"MR. BRADY:—I hereby authorize Mrs. Keckley to request my bill from you; also my goods.

16*

An exact account must be given of everything, and all goods unsold returned to me. Pray hand Mrs. Keckley my bill, without fail, immediately.

"Respectfully,

"Mrs. Lincoln."

"Saturday, Feb. 29.

"Dear Lizzie :—I am only able to sit up long enough to write you a line and enclose this check to Mr. K. Give it to him when he gives you up my goods, and require from him an exact inventory of them. I will write you to-morrow. The hour you receive this go to him, get my goods, and do not *give him the check until* you get the goods, and be sure you get a receipt for the check from him. * * In his account given ten days since, he said we had borrowed $807; now he writes for $820. Ask him what this means, and get him to deduct the $13. I cannot understand it. A letter received from K. this morning says if the check is not received the first of the

week, my goods *will be sold;* so do delay not
an hour to see him. *   * My diamond ring
he writes has been sold; the goods sold have
amounted to $824, and they appropriate all this
for their expenses. A precious set, truly. My
diamond ring itself cost more than that sum, and
I charged them not to sell it under $700. Do
get my things safely returned to me. * * * *

"Truly,

"M. L."

CPSIA information can be obtained at www.ICGtesting.com
Printed in the USA
BVOW082306030912

299379BV00001B/1/P